GOD'S
PURPOSE
FOR BIBLE PROPHECY

Robert A McLeod

WestBow
PRESS
A DIVISION OF THOMAS NELSON

GOD'S PURPOSE FOR BIBLE PROPHECY

WestBow Press books may be ordered through booksellers or by contacting:

WestBow Press
A Division of Thomas Nelson
1663 Liberty Drive
Bloomington, IN 47403
www.westbowpress.com
1-(866) 928-1240

ISBN: 978-1-4497-8002-9 (sc)
ISBN: 978-1-4497-8003-6 (hc)
ISBN: 978-1-4497-8001-2 (e)

Library of Congress Control Number: 2012923858

Printed in the United States of America

WestBow Press rev. date: 2/11/2013

TABLE OF CONTENTS

Acknowledgements vii

Introduction ix

Chapter 1: The Case for Prophecy 1

Chapter 2: Prophecy at Work in Well-Known Bible Stories 26

Chapter 3: The Four Elements of Prophecy 40

Chapter 4: The Prophecy of Jonah 47

Chapter 5: The Woman at the Well 54

Chapter 6: Remember Egypt 58

Chapter 7: Preparations from Prophecy 68

Chapter 8: Satan's Purpose for Prophecy 76

Chapter 9: Thus Says the Lord 98

Chapter 10: The Loving Parent 102

Chapter 11: Can We Know God's Purpose for Prophecy? 106

Chapter 12: The Purpose for Prophecy 110

Chapter 13: God's Glory, Our Benefit 137

Chapter 14: The Covenant Relationship 147

Chapter 15: Prophetic Prayers...155

Chapter 16: How to Study Bible Prophecy with Purpose............164

Chapter 17: The Conclusion..175

About the Author...189

Footnotes..193

ACKNOWLEDGEMENTS

Usually in an introduction there are certain acknowledgments made. Credit is given to sources of information the author drew upon in order to write their book. I have almost no sources outside of the Bible other than the inspiration of the Holy Spirit. Often authors give references from books supporting their book's research, but again, my references come mostly from the Bible. There are many books on the end times, and writers of those books have many other books from which to draw as a source of information to interpret and apply the Word of God. There were no previously written opinions and no Bible school classes from which to gather a body of information to write these books. There was no model for me to follow or anyone to consult so I could be tutored on this subject. There was no familiarity with the subject, no group of experts to consult, and no well of information to delve into to draw material to write this book. Hence, there are almost no acknowledgments to list in a convergence of footnotes.

As I wrote, I simply asked my wife Carol to read what I had just written to see if it made sense to her. She should be blessed for the many times she put up with me asking her to read something I had just learned and written while it was still raw and unrefined. She deserves credit for all her patience. She was also the one who reined me in during conversations with others when I didn't realize I had gone too far talking with someone who didn't want to talk about this aspect of prophecy. At times she would discreetly let me know that I had gone on too long when talking with someone and that I should conclude talking about it. I'm sure that I'm like others who have written books and have the subject matter readily on our minds. We don't always realize we are talking to the disinterested, the disenfranchised, or the disillusioned.

I also have solid Bible reading friends with whom I would check in with my doctrine. They were my system of checks and balances against false teaching. My doctrine may sound so rudimentary without clear scholarly backup and the mention here of much technical and educated support, but there were no established experts on this part of prophecy. I had to accept the wisdom of God and not the abundance of education that no flesh may glory in His presence. I will boast in the Lord.

On the cover is a Hubble Space Telescope image of the Pistol Star and cloud nebula. It is one of the brightest stars in our galaxy, shining brighter than ten million of our suns. Its radiance is hidden behind a cloud of dust. The Pistol Star is twenty five thousand light years away in the core of our Milky Way galaxy. Its wonders were hidden in near obscurity until the Hubble revealed its glory. We do not yet see the brilliance of God's glory yet, but one day we will stand before Him and gaze upon all His glory. Thanks to NASA for this amazing image of God's creation.

INTRODUCTION

This is a book about Bible prophecy. Now I know what you are thinking: *If this is a book about prophecy, it must be about the end times or last days.* It is important to say first that this book is *not* about the end-times prophecies. This is a much different book about Bible prophecy. It is a book about God's purpose for all Bible prophecy. His purpose for prophecy, as you will see, is much different than what our purpose for prophecy has become. Our purpose for Bible prophecy has been to take the end-times Scriptures, interpret them, and then apply them to a timetable and current events and come up with a scenario of how the earth will come to an end. God's purpose for prophecy is much greater than that. God has put prophecy into His Word to give us many advantages for our life of faith in Him.

As much as twenty seven percent of all the verses in the Bible are prophetic [1]. There are 8300 verses in your Bible that are predictive. There are 900 prophecies in the Bible concerning the second coming of Jesus [2]. As you will see there are very few prophecy-free zones in the Bible.

Most of the Bible was written by men who were prophets. The very first person in the Bible to be called a prophet was Abraham almost 3,900 years ago. Moses was a prophet because he spoke for God as shown in Exodus 7:1-2. Moses wrote the first five books of the bible and prophesied of the coming Messiah in Deuteronomy 18:15 over 1,450 years before Jesus was born. First and Second Samuel were written by the prophet Samuel. King David was a prophet and he prophesied the coming of Jesus in Psalms 2:7-9, 16:10, 22:16-18, 110:4 and 118:22. First and second Chronicles and Ezra were written by Ezra the scribe and all three books contain prophecy and fulfillment. Then there are seventeen books of the Bible written by prophets including Isaiah, Jeremiah, Ezekiel and Daniel. The four gospels record Jesus' life and in those four gospels Jesus fulfilled referenced and spoke about the future often. Jesus fulfilled over one hundred prophecies regarding the Messiah. He referenced 125 Old Testament prophecies [3] and He spoke of things to come. Paul took three missionary journeys and wrote 13 New Testament books and he wrote down many prophecies in those books. The book of Hebrews speaks a lot about prophecy although the author is unknown possibly being Barnabas, Paul's companion on his missionary journeys. James prophecies in the fifth chapter of his book to the Jews scattered abroad. Peter prophecies in his two epistles about the coming of the Lord. The apostle John wrote three short epistles and he wrote the most prophecy filled book of the Bible-Revelation.

Why did God put so much prophecy in the Bible? What did God intend for that much prophecy to do? Do Bible prophecies other than the last-days prophecies have anything to offer for our faith today? I say absolutely yes! There is so much for us to learn from the Lord when we see His purpose for prophecy. Do we need to come to God and learn to be close to Him? Do we need endurance in our faith? Do we need help in our witnessing? The answer is a resounding yes! Bible prophecy helps to bring us to Christ and provides the endurance in our faith with a special prophecy-generated ingredient called hope. It also equips us in our witnessing. All three things are essentials for our faith in Christ, and all of them come from prophecy. I believe this three-book series will show that there are indispensable and powerful things God intended for us to receive from the words He speaks about the future.

Stuck in a Rut

The mere mention of the word *prophecy* induces many responses. Most of those responses have been preconditioned by the way in which people have interacted with prophecy for the last forty years. The church has had a rather narrow view of prophecy for that length of time. That view comes from the popularity of Bible prophecies on the end times. We have such an enormous focus on that small portion of prophecy today. Our exclusion of all other Bible prophecy to focus on just the end times comes from a desire to know what the future will bring. That in itself in not bad, it is God's word and it is good to know what the Lord says will come. But we need to see all Bible prophecy to see what God is doing with it. The church today is lacking a view that defines God's purpose for all Bible prophecy. Surely we have many people who think it is cool to learn about the end times, people who avoid it, others who are confused by it and still others who have fear because of it.

The majority of Christians are not experts on the end times, and there may be some confusion regarding doctrine because we often listen to differing opinions on this controversial subject. There are differing opinions about what the future holds for the church and for individual Christians. All of these opinions sound scripturally supported and well argued, but who knows for sure which one is right? Determining who may have the correct doctrine is impossible for the average believer in the church today. Our personal beliefs tend to be swayed by the most scholarly or the most forcefully argued, or maybe we believe a certain way based on what we were taught from the beginning of our faith and have never questioned it just because it sounds right.

Most Christians are interested in the timing of the rapture because what you believe about when we are raptured determines whether you might have fear or peace about the end times. The timing of the rapture is central for believers in the end of the world. If you believe we will be raptured out of this world before the great tribulation (pre-trib), then you also believe the church will escape all the horrors of the apocalypse.

If you believe the timing of the rapture takes place in the middle of the great tribulation (mid-trib), then you will see some of the horrors of the very end of the end times. If you believe the rapture is placed at the end of that great tribulation (post-trib), then you believe you will suffer all the death and destruction the end times have to offer.

The problem with all this is that the average Christian knows they could be wrong in what they believe about the timing of the rapture. Because most believers are not experts on the end-times most would say I hope I'm raptured out of here before the great tribulation. The problem stems from hearing conflicting and well argued views. Maybe you have heard some contradicting views about the last days and wonder what the Bible really says about the Antichrist, a one-world government, the mark of the beast, and the timing of the rapture.

Some Christians who believe the church may go through some or all of the great tribulation know that without the mark of the beast, you will not be able to buy or sell anything. Their response to that is kind of like the response Egypt had to Joseph's interpretation to Pharaoh's dream, and that was to store all the grain they could in the seven years of plentiful harvests. Christians today respond by becoming more self-sufficient, buying non-perishable food, storing water, and so on in anticipation of not being able to buy anything during the apocalypse. A few spend huge sums of money to prepare for what they perceive as doomsday. They struggle to make preparations and buy enough now to be able to live then. Often the motivation for so much preparation is driven by the fear of being without in a time of need. So we often short circuit our faith when we fall into fearing what the end times may bring.

Do all the end-times prophecies really build up our faith in the Lord, or does it cause fear, confusion, and repulsion in many believers? I think it is a mixed bag with many believers in both camps. The more I preach about God having a purpose for prophecy, the more folks I encounter who are confessing a fear of the end times. The whole process of the end times is horrific, but the good news is that there are a lot of benefits God intended for His people than just debating the timing of the rapture or being afraid of the end times. We must look to see not only why God put prophecy in there but what benefits God intended for us to receive from it. There is a lot of prophecy in the Bible that has nothing to do with the end times. Today the rest of Bible prophecy is not being looked at because the end-times theology dominates most of the books, Bible studies, and preaching on prophecy. Today there are books on prophecy, there are Bible studies, and there is a lot of preaching in some churches on prophecy. There are people and churches who conduct seminars and retreats to teach their ideas of how the end times will happen.

Because there is so much talk about the end-times most Christians believe that we are coming down to the end of all things, we just have some disagreements over how the end will play out. Depending on your belief about the timing of the rapture, you may think you will be going through the time the Bible describes as the apocalypse. This is scary to many in church today. The Bible describes some pretty horrible things that will happen to people of faith in that time.

The evidence is all around us that the world is coming to its inevitable end. Some in the church cite the re-establishment of the nation of Israel almost two thousand years after it was destroyed as a major fulfillment of Bible prophecy pointing to the end-times. We have seen morals decaying and evil prospering. Christians can cite the removal of prayer and the Bible from public education, the rise of worldwide persecution of Christians, and many other things to conclude that we are living in a transitional time of deepening unrighteousness leading to the time of the apocalypse. It is in our DNA of faith, and indeed, we can find many Scriptures in the Bible to support this belief. It is because of all this that we believe things will get worse and the end is near. Individual liberties will continue to erode, and there will be a sharp polarization between good and evil, as Jesus said, "Yea the time cometh, that whosoever killeth you will think he doeth God service." John 16:2.

I will tell you that I have talked with many believers who fear this time that is coming, when simple faith in Jesus will become a death sentence. Many wonder, "Will I have the faith to endure to the end?" We know there are many believers around the world who at present are heavily persecuted for their faith in Jesus. There are nations that ban churches, make it illegal to preach Christianity, and imprison believers for their faith. Honest, Bible-believing Christians are systematically tortured, beaten, and killed for their faith. Homes, churches, and businesses belonging to Christians are set ablaze. Christians' employment is terminated, and people are heavily pressured to give up their Christian faith. It is easy to believe based on the current situation in the world and on the Scriptures that the end is near.

It is no wonder that some in the church fear the very things the Bible tells us about how the end will play out. This fear is a result of the focus the church has had on this particular aspect of prophecy for a generation. All the doom and gloom of the end times has been a scary sore spot for many. Some Christians try to avoid listening to it in their churches by helping out with the kids in Sunday school or by staying home while the subject runs its course in a Bible study the pastor is teaching. It is kind of like a factory that takes in raw materials to make something and puts out a finished product. The raw material we take in is the horrors of the end and the product that comes out is fear. It is time to change this.

This book had to be written to let people know that prophecy is more about relationship between you and God than the end times. It is not just a producer of fear or a doctrine focused on all the bad things that will come. Believers need a new direction with prophecy because prophecy is more than differing doctrines about when the rapture may happen. Prophecy was designed by God to be a faith builder, not a fear builder. This book had to be written to let every believer know there are important, basic essentials for our faith that come from prophecy. Without prophecy, our faith—indeed, even world history—would look unrecognizably different than we know it today. If you fear what the end may bring or if you are in the prophecy-disdaining group, then this book is for you.

My Own View Had to Change

I always knew there was a lot of prophecy in the Bible. Even though I studied and taught on the last days prophecies for years, I knew there must be more to it. For years I heard differing estimates of how much prophecy was in the Bible, and once I heard that prophecy made up over a quarter of all Bible verses. After that, I started wondering about it. I started asking the Lord why He might've filled up so much of His Word with things that were prophetic. That questioning was not because of doubt but because I sought to learn the answers. Eventually it led me to write these three books.

It has been a long process and a steep learning curve. As I kept seeking the Lord for answers, I began to have a new understanding about prophecy; an understanding that I had never had the slightest clue about before. This new understanding gave me a view of prophecy from God's perspective and showed me His intent for it. Certainly things from God are good for us. His Word is good for us. "His word is a lamp unto our feet" (Ps. 119:105). The goodness of the Word and the light of that lamp include a lot of words about the future.

God didn't put prophecy in the Bible to cause fear and confusion. He must have a purpose for it, and that purpose will be good for us. As I studied the issue, I realized that God had a purpose for all Bible prophecy and that purpose started to open up. I began to see prophecy in verses I had never before considered prophetic because I was starting to look for God's purpose for prophecy instead of just trying to study the end times. It was a totally different perspective to learn from. I was looking at this portion of the Scriptures with a new view; well, it was very new for me. For me it has been an amazing journey of discovery. I have learned about how God loves us and equips us to not only birth faith in Him but to energize us and spread His Word throughout the earth.

I must admit to you that I often questioned why this word came through me. I struggled greatly with why God wasn't using a well-known and respected Christian author or preacher to bring this word to the church. I certainly don't have the educational background to write a book, let alone three books on the subject. At times I felt resoundingly disqualified from writing a book about prophecy. I thought that if the Lord was showing me these things, then surely at least one well-respected and widely known Christian author or preacher was being shown the same things. It seemed so obvious that God would have a purpose for prophecy. I fully expected that while I was in the middle of writing this book, I would go into a Christian bookstore and find a new book in the prophecy section from a well-known figure in the body of Christ about God's purpose for Bible prophecy, and that would be the end of all my study and writing. I would buy that book, bring it home, read it, and gain a better understanding of prophecy than the little I had learned and written based upon my own study.

There are only two reasons I can think of that have addressed my doubts about why God has used me to bring this message. The first reason is that the Lord felt it was time for all of us to move on and learn new things from His Word about prophecy. It is possible that He was been waiting patiently for us to see the whole picture of prophecy and to give understanding to the church for the purpose of glorifying Himself and showing His love for us more clearly. The second reason is that I just asked the question of why there was so much prophecy in the Bible. I continued to seek the Lord on this, and the answers and the words kept coming. Certainly there is no special closeness or relationship I have with the Lord over anyone else in the body of Christ to receive this word from God. My faith in Christ is just like anyone else who believes in Jesus as his or her Lord and Savior. God started me on a learning curve experience in my own understanding of prophecy to write not just one book but three books on this subject. It was like the opening of a flood gate. There was a lot of information waiting for the person who sought it out.

I remember that there was a story within a movie where a lion was stalking and killing people in a village in Africa. A man saw the lion, picked up a big rock, and threw it at the lion. The rock struck the lion on the head and killed it. The village was so excited that the lion was dead that they made the man a leader in that village. He marveled that he had become the leader of his village because of what he had done. He said, "I just threw a rock." He didn't think what he had done was very special. Like that man, I don't think what I have done is that special; I just asked the questions. Rather, what the Lord has done is very special.

I confess it has been a humbling learning experience to learn about His purpose for prophecy. Everything I have studied about the last days has taken a backseat to seeing the Lord's love for me. I thought I knew my doctrine well concerning prophecy, yet everything I knew and taught about prophecy wasn't worth much at all compared to the riches of knowing Him personally. I kept trying to study end-times prophecy, and the Lord kept showing me His love. The Holy Spirit kept showing me how much I am loved by pointing out the prophetic Scriptures I was studying to show me His great love.

I realized that God was revealing His desire for me to be close to Him through the prophecy I was studying. I had humbling moments at the computer when the Lord kept showing me His great love as I learned more and more about the way He loves me and embraces me, not only through prophetic verses but through all His words in the Bible. I admit

I was too thick headed at first to understand what God was showing me. I just didn't get it at first because—well, I had taught this stuff for years. I had labored in the Word and listened to sermons on it, and I had confidence in what I knew about prophecy. Basically I thought I had this prophecy stuff all figured out and the Lord didn't need to teach me anything else about it. I wouldn't have said that out loud, but through my pride and arrogance, that was what I was thinking. The Lord took all that away by showing me His great love through prophecy. Of course, I don't want to be so subject-singular when it comes to His love. He shows His remarkable love in many other ways too.

I listen to radio and TV preachers all the time, but I have never heard one sermon or read one chapter in a book on prophecy saying a word about God having a purpose for using so much prophecy in His Word or about what God has foretold of the benefits for a person who lives a life of faith in Christ being based on prophecy. I have never heard anything saying that God's promises start as prophecy or that our promised inheritance is based in prophecy. It may have been seldom said, but it is true nonetheless. There may be pastors and teachers who teach about this side of prophecy, but it must be rare because I have never heard anyone speak about it. It seems like everyone who has taught or written on prophecy has followed the same wagon in front of them in book after book and sermon after sermon by taking the end-times prophecies, interpreting, and applying them to current events to produce their doctrine.

I have read some of the prefaces of books on prophecy that include a definition of prophecy, but they do not tell of a purpose for prophecy and why God put so much of it into His Word. Most of those prefaces will say that God wants us to know what will happen, that is true but there is much more to it than that. I'm sure someone will point out a sermon or chapter of a book after the publication of these books that will show someone who talked or wrote about this aspect of prophecy, but in my experience, I have never heard or seen it.

Recently I was watching TV, and there was an advertisement for the next show, saying it was about Bible prophecy. I continued to watch as the show came on. The preacher appeared and began to talk about how the end times were about to happen on the world stage. Of course, he had his own explanation about how he thought things would happen. There are pastors who teach a series on prophecy, and there are conferences, lectures, and retreats that teach on the subject of the end times. The current format of interpretation and application of the Scriptures about the end times is a well-worn path for a generation. It is almost like we have locked up our doctrine and only let prophecy be viewed as relating to the end times. Christian bookstore shelves have many end times–themed books on the situation on the Middle East, the great tribulation, the new temple, the Antichrist, the one-world government, the rapture, the mark of the beast, financial meltdowns, Armageddon, and an idea of how all these events play out. All of those subjects about the end times are okay to teach on, but somehow the church has mislaid the most important aspect of prophecy. We suffer as individual believers as a result of not knowing its purpose or understanding and enjoying its benefits.

At times, many fellow believers in the church didn't understand what I was writing about because prophecy was so ingrained in them that they could only understand it in the context of the end times. Many times I would mention some aspect about God having a purpose for prophecy and would get blank stares. There would be times when I started to talk about God's purpose for prophecy, and some preprogrammed believers would put their hands up in a stop motion and say, "Sorry, I'm not into that stuff." The church has programmed them to think of prophecy as only being about the end times. They thought I was going to start talking about the battle of Armageddon, the mark of the beast, or the great tribulation, and they weren't going to listen to all that death and destruction from a doctrine that seems to be fed by too many energy drinks. They have issues stemming from past negative experiences regarding prophecy, and they didn't want to ever go there again. I understand the difficulty that some righteous people in the church have with prophecy as it has been portrayed today.

I greatly sympathize with Christians who feel this way. I understand for the last forty years, the church has presented a very narrow view of the whole picture of prophecy. It is like an action-adventure, shoot-'em-up movie, and it has been playing in the theaters for the past forty years. There are no movies in the theaters about love, tenderness, feelings, and relationships. The same movie is still playing over and over again. It shows death and destruction, lots of shooting, lots of explosions, and car chase after car chase. It is difficult to see understanding, love, and close personal relationships in a movie like this. But some of us keep lining up outside the movie theaters to see it again and again.

Christians who were avid readers of the Bible were the only ones who took what I had learned, started to put it together, and said, "Well, that fits with this, and that fits with that." They would say they had never considered looking at prophecy that way, but it fit with Scripture. I looked forward to discussing what I felt God was showing me with them and hearing their ideas about what I was writing. It was my system of checks and balances so I wasn't alone in my doctrine.

This book is the first of its kind on the subject of Bible prophecy, and as such, it breaks new ground in our understanding on this part of God's Word. I sense that the Lord is delighted to give us this insight from His Word. He wants us to know Him and be more closely in tune with what He has spoken in His Word. Don't we know the Lord through His Word and through what the Holy Spirit is teaching us? This book takes Bible prophecy in a new direction; at least it is new for the church today. I believe the first-century knew about prophecy in ways we don't often understand today because we only understand it in one context—the end times. The church of today is like an old vinyl record playing on a record player with the needle stuck on one of the tracks of the record. It keeps playing the same short segment of the record over and over again. Maybe God is lifting the needle out of its track and setting it down just past the place where it was skipping so we can go on in our understanding of the Bible.

This book is for everyone in the church today. It is for those who have had enough of the death and destruction side of the last-days prophecies as they have been preached on and written about for over a generation. I really do understand believers' disdain for and difficulty with prophecy as it is portrayed today. This book is for the person who is confused by all the differing opinions and the controversy it generates.

This book will not sort out all the differing views about the last days, but it will offer insight into the nature of God by looking at reason behind His use of so much prophecy in His Word to us. It is for the person who believes he or she has a handle on end-times doctrine and who wants to learn more about prophecy. No, this book will not give conclusive proof on difficult-to-interpret passages on Bible prophecy, such as determining the exact location of Tarshish in Ezekiel 38. It will not be talking about a role, if any, that America might play in the last days. This book will add a new dimension to your understanding of prophecy. It is for those who fear going through the horrors of the apocalypse and who wonder if they will be able to stand for Christ when simple faith in Jesus may cost them their lives. This book will give them a look at the loving nature of our Lord through all Bible prophecy, and that may give them strength to go through any tough time that may come their way.

This view of prophecy unites us and helps us to see many things about the Lord that are good for us. It shows us the basis for many benefits for our faith. It is simple: Bible prophecy is for everyone because God designed Bible prophecy to benefit every believer's faith.

I apologize right now for being a bit repetitious in this and the following two books, but the repetition will help with the reprogramming in our understanding of prophecy. Repetition is good to help us learn something new, especially when we have learned something in only one way. I know that American auto mechanics learning about American-made cars have to go through a long, complicated learning process to learn the procedures to take apart and fix an engine. Experienced mechanics know the engine well, and they know those procedures well for the American-made brand they are working on. But give these mechanics Japanese or German-made engines to take apart, and they will be at a loss. They will have to learn all-new procedures particular to those engines. Certainly some procedures might be the same, but mechanics have to keep learning and being reminded that there are new and different ways of working with a foreign engine. It is the same with our view of prophecy. This book will challenge your perception of prophecy to bring you into a new understanding of what God is doing with His words about the future.

My hope for this book and the two that follow is that many people will see God glorified, and in seeing Him glorified, they will come to a saving knowledge of Jesus Christ and gain a deeper understanding of Him and the love He has for us. It is also my hope that these books will unite the church, give our faith endurance by strengthening our hope in Christ, and spread the gospel. I believe there are many treasures of understanding awaiting your discovery. Our God is so amazing and diverse. We will forever be awed and humbled by His majesty and power.

What Is Bible Prophecy?

Bible prophecy is very, very simple. God knows the future, and He tells us about it in the Bible. We do not know what will happen one minute or one thousand years from now. It is when we see a fulfillment of a word God has spoken come true that we have a realization of His existence. When we understand that He exists, we are drawn to know the God who knows the future. God created and designed prophecy to bring us into relationship with Him. John 6:44 says, "No man can come to me except the Father which hath sent me draw him: and I will raise him up at the last day." A good portion of the way in which the Father draws us is by getting prophecy into us through reading the Bible. Prophecy is like the hook on the end of a fishing line. Once we take the bait on the hook, the Father reels us in into relationship with Jesus.

Bible prophecy instructs, gives vision, has directed ministry, builds trust, and glorifies God. Prophetic fulfillment is the principal way in which the faithfulness of God is displayed. Most importantly of all, prophetic fulfillment reaches out to everyone to prove God exists so that we are drawn to believe in God and to turn faith and trust into relationship. The end times is a beginning to understand prophecy, but it was never meant to be the only place we go with prophecy. The church must go on to discover the essentials and indeed the riches that prophecy offers to everyone.

Looking with Blinders On

Imagine going to the Louvre Museum in Paris and looking at its Renaissance collection of paintings. In the Louvre, you can gaze upon many of the paintings that were painted by the great masters—Leonardo Da Vinci, Michelangelo, Raphael, and many more. The Renaissance-era paintings are acclaimed to be some of the greatest paintings ever painted.

As you go through that great museum, you start to focus on one painting in particular. As you stand before this painting, you closely examine this beautiful painting, but as you study it, you start to focus on only one small part of that painting. Soon you are ignoring the rest of the work the artist did on that canvas. Surely the one part of the painting that you are fixed upon was painted by the great master, but you ignore the rest to focus on the smaller part of the canvas. Others come up to the painting, and you show them what you are looking at, and they too focus on that small portion of the painting. Soon everyone focuses on that one small part of the painting. Reproductive copies are printed, not of the whole painting but just of the smaller piece everyone is fixed upon. There are books written, lectures and seminars that teach about it, and all the people talk only about that smaller portion of the famous painting. That smaller part of the painting is so popular that everyone forgets about the rest of the painting. It has become impossible to remember a time long ago when everyone looked at and took in the whole picture.

Of course you would say that is ridiculous, but that situation with the painting is the same as the church's current relationship with prophecy. For the past forty years, our view of biblical prophecy has been mostly confined to the end times, and we have ignored the very purpose of prophecy. For a generation we have taken the end-times prophecies, interpreted them, and then applied them to current events. We have come up with a doctrine that reflects only the last-days portion of prophecy. That is a narrow part of the whole picture of prophecy. There is much more to see, to know, and to experience from the whole picture of biblical prophecy. There are important things that our faith misses out on when we focus on only a small part of prophecy and ignore God's purpose for it.

As wonderful as it is to know God's words about the future and how events in the future may affect us, there are more benefits in knowing His purpose for prophecy. Our lives can be filled with the wonderful and powerful advantages that a proper understanding of prophecy brings into the life of the believer. God has a purpose for prophecy, and these books were written to show that purpose. God has a vital purpose for prophecy, with many indispensable benefits for those who live their lives in faith. Without biblical prophecy, our faith would look much different than it does now. Indeed, we would be living in a much different world than we know now. Let's go on in our understanding of prophecy to enjoy the benefits that are available right now.

God's purpose for Bible prophecy can be summed up in this way: By prophecy God does something that we can't do—telling the future—so that when we see the fulfillment come, we realize that He exists and are drawn to know more about Him in faith and trust, and the result is relationship. Fulfilled prophecy proves God and provokes faith. We have no capacity to know the future; God retained that unique ability for Himself when He created us. When we hear words about the future and see their fulfillment, we are confronted with the reality that God must exist because man cannot know the future by himself.

How can something that does not exist inspire someone to tell the future? How can that predicted future happen exactly the way it was predicted when man does not even know what the next minute will bring? If God is not real, then someone fulfilled all the prophecy in the Bible on their own. There are about a thousand prophecies in the Bible. Why would generations of people for thousands of years go about to speak and then fulfill prophecy on their own? Isaiah's prophecy of a virgin conceiving and bearing a son (Isa. 7:14) was fulfilled seven hundred years after it was spoken. If man were to fulfill that prophecy, you would have to pass on that deception to your descendants for seven hundred years and then select someone to fulfill it. You would have to convince a young Jewish boy to die an excruciating execution on a cross at an early age. It takes more faith to believe in that nonsense than it does to believe in the living God.

The truth here is that words about the future and their fulfillment prove God exists. God loaded up His Word with those words about the future to offer overwhelming proof to you that He exists so that when we see a prophecy in the Bible come to be fulfilled, it causes faith to be born and to grow. God related so much of His Word in a way that tells the future to create and deepen relationship with everyone, to strengthen your hope, and to empower your witness to the world.

Over one quarter of all Bible verses have prophetic content. That high a percentage of Bible Scripture being prophetic may surprise most Christians. There are over thirty-one thousand verses in the Bible; that translates to over eight thousand verses in the Bible that are prophetic.

We read a lot of prophecy when we read the Bible. Often when we read Bible prophecy, we don't realize prophecy is there on the pages of our Bibles because it doesn't identify itself first with that well-known prophetic introduction, "Thus saith the Lord." We have all read and heard how the Bible prophets spoke those words before speaking for God.

Jesus spoke a lot of prophecy without ever saying that phrase first. He said in Matthew 5:5, "Blessed are the meek: for they shall inherit the earth." We all know that famous portion of Scripture. We call those eight verses out of Matthew are known as the Beatitudes because they are about people of faith who have certain qualities and who will receive certain blessings and rewards. Did you know that the Beatitudes are prophetic? Those who are meek, the merciful, the pure in heart, peacemakers, and those who are persecuted for righteousness sake do not have their rewards yet because they are all future benefits for those believers who have those qualities or for those who suffer persecution. Jesus didn't use the prophetic declaration "Thus saith the Lord" when He spoke those blessings upon those believers, but the Beatitudes are prophecies taking the form of promises for the future.

Book Two

The second book in this three-book series on biblical prophecy is about promises and hope. All promises in the Bible that relate to our inheritance in Christ had their start as a prophecy. God makes some fantastic promises to people of faith. The promises originate in prophecy. Those promises give us an expectancy of receiving what has been promised. Consider that our hope in Christ is not a vague term, like an abstract painting, which can easily have many opposing interpretations. Our hope in Christ is real. It is a clear doctrine, and it lives to empower us in our faith. Take away hope from our lives of faith, and our whole Christian experience is only a shadow of what it was intended to be. It all begins when God speaks a word about the future. It may be that the Lord spoke it Himself, such as when He talked with Abraham, Jacob, or Moses, or He may've spoken the word through a prophet like Isaiah or Ezekiel. The Lord Jesus may've taught on it, or maybe in one of the letters one of the disciples wrote prophecies about it. The word about the future becomes a promise, which in turn gives us our hope in Christ.

We can talk about things we will do, but our words about what we will do don't automatically become promises like God's words do. We know that all of God's words about the future will come to pass, but only a smaller portion of those words become the promises that make up our inheritance in Christ. Those very special words are promises that generate our hope. Those promises are the standard of God's words about our future with Him. Those prophetic words that become promises that give us hope. The benefits of faith that are received when we meet the Lord face to face are contained in only a small portion of prophecy, yet they are a very powerful motivator to help us endure our life of faith. Fantastic things are promised to us because we have decided to have faith in Jesus. These promises give a strong and enduring hope that empowers kingdom service and a greater strength to crucify our flesh, lose our life for Christ, and become the living sacrifices that He intended. Would you say that those things are essentials for our faith? Of course, it is obvious, and prophecy is the basis that gives us those essentials

Think of when you have promised to do something or change something. Promises are made to do something in the future. The person you make the promise to hopes that you keep your promise because he or she will benefit from you keeping the promise. It is the same way in our relationship with the Lord. How powerful a motivator is it to know that God promises us eternal life with Him as a result of our faith? How much benefit is there for our faith in knowing that Jesus is preparing a place for us in heaven right now? How does it affect us now to know that God will give us new, eternal bodies that never feel pain? These words and many more are prophesied words that transform into our promised inheritance and are obtained by our faith in Christ. These are the very things that make up our hope in Christ, the fantastic things God will give us for our faith in Him.

Book Three

The third and final book in the series on prophecy is about evangelism. What may surprise many people is that the Holy Spirit has led the way using prophecy in evangelism. Bible prophecy is highly evangelical. The Bible contains many examples of using prophecy in evangelism to prove God is real and jump-start relationship. God uses His words about the future as His own evangelism to reach out to everyone to show that He is real and to produce faith and trust. It is God's heart to reach everyone and that none should perish. Many times the way in which He reaches out to prove Himself and create faith is by prophecy. Prophecy is involved in many Bible stories to change hearts from unbelief to faith and to follow the Lord.

Three Parts

It is beyond amazement that prophecy is so relational when we look to see God's purpose for it. What you will learn about prophecy here will transform you; it transformed me. The transformation is good, and it is growth in our walk with Jesus.

It could be said that there are three parts to God's purpose for prophecy. First, the purpose is to create relationship, as this book will show. It reaches out to us, proving that God is real. Only God can tell the future, so when we see a prophecy come to fulfillment, it shows us He exists. Once we recognize God's existence, we have a decision to make. Fulfilled Bible prophecy forces us to make a decision, either to start faith or start denying what happened as a coincidence or say that people fulfilled that word about the future on their own. People can make up all sorts of fanciful explanations of fulfilled prophecy to deny it has come from God. The prime motivator to deny it comes from their love of sin and lack of desire to change. If the decision is made to follow the Lord, then faith has been born.

Second, Bible prophecy fills us up with the power of hope. Never underestimate the power of hope in your life of faith with Jesus. It is the power that keeps you going in your faith. The things we place our hope in are fantastic promises of things we will receive as a result of our faith. Those promises are rooted deeply in prophecy, like that verse from Matthew, "Blessed are the meek; for they shall inherit the earth." "For they shall inherit the earth," is a future event that has not happened, yet it is a generator of hope to those of us who are meek to receive the whole world as a part of their inheritance from Jesus.

Third, we are sent forth to the world equipped with Bible prophecy to prove God to the world. If God's purpose for all Bible prophecy is to prove Himself to the world for the purpose of creating relationship, then we can use it that way too. There are many examples in the Bible of the prophets, Jesus, the apostles, and the Holy Spirit using prophecy in evangelism to create fellowship with God. God has done everything He has done to bring us into a tender and close relationship with Him.

We Just Can't Do It

Knowing the future by prophecy motivates Christians to purify themselves in their faith. It motivates us by knowing there is an end to all things, followed by a judgment for the way we lived our lives. It provides the ultimate accountability of eternal damnation or eternal reward. Even the fear of hell brings people to faith all the time, but the most important purpose that prophecy serves is to bring you to God and to deepen your relationship with Him.

We come to faith by prophecy by seeing that He exists, like Hebrews 11:6 says: "But without faith it is impossible please him; for he that cometh to God must believe that he is, and that he is a rewarder of them that diligently seek him." It is by prophecy that God proves He exists because humankind has no ability whatsoever to tell the future. When God made the blueprint for humankind, He didn't include in the design the capacity for humans to know the future. It is by doing something that we cannot do that God proves He is real to bring us to faith.

Please understand that true and accurate words about the future are rare and precious and come from God. We come to God knowing that He is, like Hebrews 11:6 says, but we come because God is proving who He is by the constant testimony of prophetic fulfillment in the Bible. Understand that only fulfilled prophecy proves God is real. Fulfillment of prophecy is the proof of His existence. End-times prophecies have largely not yet been fulfilled yet, so they do not prove God is real. The long record of past fulfilled Bible prophecies assures us that prophecies in the Bible that are as yet unfulfilled will also come to pass in time.

We can try to tell the future, but we just don't have that capacity. There have been too many false prophets throughout time who tried very hard to see the future and make their predictions. If we stretch it quite a bit, some of their uninspired predictions have sounded like they have come true, somewhat. We live in a time when many people make many predictions about the future all the time, from weather forecasts to economic forecasts. The media has made accurate words about the future very rare by ignoring God's Word altogether. The church has made prophecy confusing by dividing ourselves into differing camps of doctrine that cause controversy. We debate the Scriptures about when and how things will happen. What pastor wants to bring that confusion and controversy into his church? So those words are best avoided by many churches today. Those words are rare because there is a lack of Bible knowledge in most of the world today.

But it is with these special words that we can reach out to a world that desperately needs the hope and love that only the Lord offers. I'm sure some people will keep trying to tell the future without the inspiration of the Holy Spirit, but we can easily identify them as the charlatans they are and avoid them. But more than just avoiding the false, we embrace those special words of truth about the future that God speaks, and those are found within the pages of the Bible. When someone hears those special words about the future and carefully examines them with an objective heart, those words can cause faith to be born. A life is transferred from death to life, and a loving relationship with God begins.

Many Facets

Bible prophecy is diverse. Prophecy has many components and functions but one main purpose. First it is by prophecy that God proves Himself by prophetic fulfillment. It is a sort of proof of His existence, and it is in this proof that we are drawn to know Him. Its purpose is to bring us close to Him as sons and daughters of His kingdom, so its purpose is relational.

When the Jews went down into Egypt and eventually were enslaved by the Egyptians, God had a plan. God let them know what that plan was by prophecy. Part of the plan of God was to birth a nation within Egypt to come out to serve Him. Two hundred years before the Jews went into Egypt, God told Abraham of His plan for His people to be in Egypt for four hundred years in hard bondage. While the Jews were in Egypt, they knew God had set a time limit on their stay in that land and then He would deliver them. When that time came and the Jews were delivered, it fulfilled the prophecy. God kept His word to the descendants of Abraham. It caused the people to come to Him in faith because He is faithful to keep His Word.

Second, the diversity of prophecy continues its benefits by the inspired words about the future that create our precious hope in Christ. When you hope for something, you are called hopeful. When you are in despair, you are called hopeless. The things we hope for in Christ are eternal life and being in heaven with Jesus. These are fantastic things that God has told us will be given to the person of faith. It is by prophecy that we understand the amazing benefits a life of faith brings to the believer. We read the words of God that promise us resurrection from the dead, receiving new bodies that never feel pain or sorrow, eternal life, and life in heaven with Jesus for eternity. It is by faith in these words about our future benefits that we can have hope.

Fantastic benefits produce a powerful and very noticeable hope. These prophetically driven promises produce our hope in Christ, and that hope enables us to endure in a life in faith. When you have a great hope, it helps you to do things that are contrary to your human nature, enabling growth in your walk with Christ and in your service and ministry to Him. The purpose of hope is to give endurance to faith. We need endurance to live our life in faith until we meet the Lord. An element of prophecy's purpose is to keep us in faith.

Some prophecies are promised rewards for faith that we will receive when we meet Jesus. Other prophecies produce vision, like looking forward to a Promised Land or returning home to your own land after predicted seventy-year captivity in a foreign land. Some prophecies have required some kind of response, exemplified by Noah's building of an ark or Egypt storing grain, Nineveh's repentance, or Mary and Joseph fleeing into Egypt to escape those trying to kill Jesus. Because of some prophecies, people of faith purify themselves. God gives all prophecy with the desire of producing faith in everyone. Some prophecies are promises that we place our hope in. Prophecy empowers our evangelism to prove that God is real and reach out to the world. Prophecy has that quality about it that beautifully colors just about every facet of our faith in the Lord.

Prophecy forms the basis of our inheritance in God. God's words about the future reach out to us to build faith and trust, and they bring us close to Him. Then the Word of God tells us (promises us) what we will receive when we meet the Lord face to face, and that motivates us to lifelong faith empowered by hope.

Prophecy is also highly evangelical. God sends us out into the world with His words about the future to show others that He is real and offer hope to others so they too will come to know Him. Prophecy properly used in evangelism reaches out to a world that desperately needs the Lord. God has used much prophecy when speaking to people in the Bible, and the Holy Spirit is active using prophecy when speaking through someone who is filled with the Spirit. Whether speaking to or through someone, the purpose is the same when those words are prophetic: to glorify Himself so that we will come to Him in relationship upon seeing the prophetic word come true.

It is a God-purposed cycle. You can see there are three parts to this cycle. First God speaks words about the future that come true, proving He exists. We see this proof and come to faith in Him, which leads to relationship. It is so simple to understand that it is kind of like driving into a gas station. You come to the gas pump, you fill up, and you go out. We come to God by prophecy, we fill up on endurance (hope) by prophecy, and we go out equipped with the very thing that drew us to Him in the first place.

Prophecy is present and active in each of the three cycles. Of course, prophecy is not the only way in which the Lord saves us, empowers us, and sends us out with His words about the future to show others the way to God. There are other means God uses to bring people to faith in Him. All prophecy, both fulfilled and unfulfilled, is a powerful impetus in a faith-based relationship with the Eternal One. It fills us up with a powerful hope to live our entire lives in faith and obedience to our King. He sends us out into the world's harvest to bring others to Him.

> But as it is written; Eye hath not seen, nor ear heard, neither
> have entered into the heart of man, the things which God hath

prepared for them that love him. But God hath revealed them unto us by his Spirit; for the Spirit searcheth all things yea, the deep things of God. (1 Cor. 2:10)

The previous verse tell us that God is preparing very special things for those who love Him. We have extreme benefits for our eternity with Christ. While the actual list of things that God has prepared for those who love Him are not listed in this verse, we know that they include many fantastic things that are future benefits for a life lived in faith.

A Lot about the Future

If it is true that one quarter of all Bible verses are about prophecy, then a question is begging to be asked of God: "Lord, why did You relate so much of Your Word in a way that tells the future?" I believe that the Bible itself gives us the answer to that question. When I think of how much prophecy is in the Bible, it makes me seek to know why it is there, and that starts me on the path to understanding God's purpose for prophecy. The Bible tells us why biblical prophecy is so crucial and beneficial to Christians today.

God put so much prophecy into His Word because He wants us to know not only know about prophecy; He wants us to know His purpose for it and to experience all the benefits that come from knowing those words He inspired men to write about the future. He lovingly wants us to be in a close relationship with Him, to have a stronger hope and a powerful way to witness of our faith, and to see His faithfulness. He wants to give us a new identity in Christ and to help us understand how much He desires relationship with us. We all pray as Christians to be closer to the Lord. We pray that prayer all the time. We move closer to the Lord in many ways, and primarily we move closer to Him when we see His great love for us. We move closer to the Lord when we understand how that love moves to lovingly bring us closer to Him, and prophecy is clearly a way that moves us closer to Him. All of this comes from ancient Bible prophecy? Yes, and more!

Prophecy is such a rich subject in the Bible. It is almost unfortunate that we ignore the riches of prophecy in favor of knowing prophecy only in the context of the end times. It is like going to the Grand Teton National Park and focusing on only one tree and ignoring the magnificence of everything else there. The tree is okay to gaze upon at—it is beautiful by itself—but there is much more to see.

The Very First Wagon

One of the very first popular books on prophecy was written over forty years ago. It was called *The Late Great Planet Earth* and was written by Hal Lindsey. For many years it was a trailblazing book in our understanding of the end times. The many books on Bible prophecy that have followed since then have pretty much followed the same theme by taking the end-times prophecies, interpreting them, and then applying them in various ways in the light of current events to produce an end-times scenario of what the authors think will happen. This process of interpretation and application of end-times Scriptures continues today. I confess that I have studied and taught pretty much in the same way as many of the writers and teachers of end times doctrine by doing the same interpreting and applying of the end-times Scriptures.

It is sort of like a long wagon train. The first wagon in front rolls across a smooth dirt road. The many wagons that follow cut ruts into the road by their wheels as they follow the wagon in front of them. Soon the ruts in that road are cut so deep that the last wagons on that wagon train have no choice but to stay in those ruts and follow the same path as every other wagon that has gone before it. Our views of prophecy today are like the wagons on that wagon train. One book was written, and all the rest have followed the trail that the first book made through the wilderness called the last days.

All the preaching, books, sermons, and Bible classes that teach on the end times have a downside in the hearts of believers. That downside is the fear and confusion that are attached to end-times teachings. Some believers have told me that they don't know what to believe and that they are afraid of the wrath to come. The death and destruction aspect of the end-times prophecies makes some of us afraid of the future. We do not know what will happen because of the conflicting doctrines. Will we go through the great tribulation, or will the Lord take us in the rapture of the church before that horrible time comes? We struggle to have trust in the Lord when we know that we will go through this horrible tribulation. It is not so much that we are in a rut with the end times, but we need to discover much more about prophecy.

The books on Bible bookstore shelves are there for anyone to read and learn about the end times. Any reader can gain an understanding about how things will play out in these times, and it is a mixed blessing to know what will happen in the future because of the fear factor. The books on the Bible bookstore shelves seem to follow a singular path in their interpretation and application of prophecy that leads to the end times.

Hear This, Think That

Interpretation and application to current events is the usual format writers and preachers take in writing and talking about end-times prophecy. We form many of our Bible doctrines that way. For the last forty years, the church has been preached to and taught by all the books that interpret and apply all the end-times Scriptures. The church has been shaped by all this for a generation. Now when we hear the word *prophecy*, we automatically think of the end times. Just ask any group of Christians if they could tell you about prophecy, and it is very likely they will start talking about the Antichrist, a one-world government, a Russian attack on Israel, the new coming temple, and Armageddon.

That singular response to prophecy is almost like the well-known

Pavlovian conditioning. Every freshman college student who has taken psychology 101 has learned about it. In Pavlovian conditioning, you have a dog, a bell, and some food. If you ring the bell each time before feeding the dog, the dog learns to associate the bell with food. Time after time the bell is rung and then the dog is fed. With that conditioning in place, the bell can be rung, and with no food or odor of any food present, the dog will salivate in anticipation of being fed. Say the word *prophecy*, and the church automatically thinks of the end times. We have been conditioned to think this way from the last forty years of conditioning from sermons, Bible studies, and books on prophecy.

It's time to break out of the rut we are in regarding prophecy. It is time to see that prophecy was also meant to be about other things that are just as important to know about as what we presently understand about the end times. I'm not saying we should forget about the end times, and I'm certainly not saying we shouldn't read any books about the end times. But we need to see more about prophecy than what we can see looking through a keyhole. It is time to take a step back and look at the whole picture.

For me the door to understanding God's purpose for prophecy was through studying the end times, so I'm very appreciative to the writers and pastors who wrote and taught about the end times. They shaped my view and helped me on my way to understanding. Maybe a wider understanding of prophecy for you will be by some other way. Wherever the entrance, enter we must.

Warning, Warning, Warning!

Many a false teaching and cult have started with one person misinterpreting some Scripture and building a doctrine and a following with it. Let me make it perfectly clear that many proponents of false doctrines have said many of the same things I have said. Someone receives a "revelation," and it becomes a doctrine people follow to their own hurt. Their doctrine violates solid Bible teaching and Scripture. The church has a long and sad history with these deceivers and their false teachings and doctrines. The test of any doctrine is that it must align with all Scripture. There is no new revelation that will change that. "Jesus Christ is the same yesterday, and today, and forever" (Heb. 13:8). If the Lord is the same all the time, then why would He say something that is different today than what He said yesterday? He will not violate His own spoken word.

If the warning flags are waving in your mind that you are about to start reading about a false doctrine, please put your mind at ease. Let the church test what I say by comparing it to all Scripture. Everything about God's purpose for prophecy points to God. It shows His great love for us, and as it will be described, it shows His faithfulness and glory. Cults and false teachings usually glorify some person and represent their interpretation of Scripture as truth and/or a revelation from God.

God's purpose for Bible prophecy is not a doctrine that will violate Scripture because it just shows what God is doing in His use of prophecy. It shows His loving and inclusive nature. It shows His desire to give us the power of hope to sustain our faith until we go home to meet Him. It shows His love for the entire world because He sends us out to preach using words that prove His existence and do good works in His name so He will be glorified and people will be drawn to Him.

The way in which cults are started is by someone having a revelation or by a misinterpretation of Scripture that creates a doctrine that is out of line with all the rest of Scripture. Usually the person who starts a cult interprets some Scripture to be about himself or herself that lifts that person up and exalts him or her. Cults almost always have exclusivity so that only the people who are in that cult are saved and everyone else in the world is going to hell. In God's purpose for prophecy, no person is exalted. It shows the benefit of being close to Jesus, and that is the best benefit of all. Keep your spiritual armor on and continue reading, but

I think you will find this is a way of looking at prophecy that will not lift up a person or espouse a new revelation. It will not violate any other Scripture, and it will point your heart toward our loving Lord.

Changed but Still the Same

There is no need for anyone to lay aside their beliefs about end times or about any prophetic interpretations to accept what this work has to say. There is no need to change any beliefs about what may or may not happen. If you are pre-trib, mid-trib, or post-trib, you can keep your view intact after reading this book. How many of our views that we think are so important now will still be left intact after we meet Him face to face? Understanding God's purpose for prophecy says more about His loving nature than any of our views. Understanding God's purpose for prophecy wonderfully supplements your view of end-times prophecy and indeed all prophecy. It is like the salt we put on our food to enliven the taste; the flavor is enhanced, but the food is the same. Understanding that God's purpose for prophecy is to bring us into an everlasting relationship is a view that will last forever because it is true.

The church today needs to see God's purpose for Bible prophecy. We'll lay aside a lot of the interpretations and applications of the usual end-times Scriptures and instead focus on the purpose for prophecy. I hope that there will be some reprogramming from the commonly known equation of prophecy equals end times. We can learn new mathematics that will teach us that prophecy equals relationship. In the second book, we will learn more new math, and we can add to that equation to say prophecy equals promises and hope. Going even further in our new math, we will see that prophecy equals evangelism, it equals vision and identity and so on. The response of the church to the first and well-known equation of prophecy equals end times is sometimes confusion, debate, and fear. Sometimes the response is to purify ourselves, knowing there is a predicted end to all things.

The response to the equation that says that Bible prophecy equals relationship is to know, understand and experience the benefits of being drawn to God for fellowship. We are drawn closer to Him when His faithfulness is displayed by fulfilling all His words about the future. That faithfulness is extreme when a word about the future is spoken and then centuries pass before it is fulfilled.

Our response to the equation that that Bible prophecy equals promises and hope is to see that prophecy is the original form of promises upon which we build our hope. Never underestimate the powerful aspect of hope in our faith. It is the part of us that keeps us going in our faith.

We respond to another equation that says Bible prophecy equals evangelism by going out into the world equipped with words from the Bible that prove God exists. We can tell the world that prophecy proves God is real, and His desire is to bring everyone into a close and loving fellowship. Also from prophecy comes our vision and direction. Prophecy shows us our true identity in Christ, motivates kingdom service, and reaches out to the world with a power-proven way to evangelize.

It is not my intention to trivialize all the end times–themed books; I taught about it for many years, and I still do, but there is a lot more to prophecy than all the coming doom and gloom. There is much more to learn about prophecy than the Antichrist, a one-world government, or Armageddon. We must round out what we know and believe about Bible prophecy to become fully mature in our understanding. We must understand why there is so much prophecy is in the Bible. Christians may debate about end-time predictions, but understanding the purpose draws us closer to God.

The debate about prophecy continues in all the end-times Scriptures if they have already been fulfilled and if Israel's existence as a nation today is just a coincidence or is a fulfillment of Bible prophecy and more that is yet to be fulfilled. We have divided ourselves into those three belief groups that relate to the timing of the rapture in relation to the great tribulation and another called amillennial. Those of us in the church who are into the subject of prophecy often divide and confuse many others in the church with our views. It is entirely possible that these differing opinions have given false doctrines a place to flourish. These differing opinions have turned off quite a few believers from seeking after prophecy. Maybe the church should have a Christian consumer of doctrine review board to review each doctrine and see which ones really hold up under close scrutiny and recommend which ones to believe in. Even then the reviewers would be looked at as biased or tainted in some way and the controversy would continue.

Debates and Confusion

A result of being stopped by this road block of confusion is that Christians are prevented from going further to know about God's wonderful purpose and the many amazing benefits He designed for us to receive from knowing His words about the future. Being mature in our understanding of the Bible and what it says about prophecy is so important to our faith and releases strength and endurance for all who know prophecy's purpose. Maturity and freedom through prophecy help to enable evangelism, reaffirm God's faithfulness, and strengthen our hope in His promises to us. Having these things through prophecy and seeing God's purpose for prophecy unifies the church and strengthens our witness to the world because God is lifted up and glorified all the more.

When we become familiar with God's purpose for prophecy, it helps us to trust God because He always knows the future and we are safe and secure in Him no matter what may come. As James says, "But the wisdom that is from above is first pure, then peaceable, gentle, and easy to be intreated, full of mercy and good fruits, without partiality, and without hypocrisy." James 3:17. Unfortunately, we don't apply this Scripture to the debates we have about the end times, much to our own hurt, but it is a point of maturity to do so. As James says, the wisdom from above is more peaceable and more easily entreated than debates and the divisions we have created.

When we endlessly debate end-times Scriptures and about what will happen, we do not see God's purpose for Bible prophecy where God is at the center of it all and He is magnified. Debating and being more knowledgeable than someone else in order to prove our point becomes our focus. Sometimes the fruit of the debates is fear. When we fear the future, it defeats faith. When we understand God's purpose for prophecy, He becomes our focus, and that is what He intended. The church has studied biblical prophecy for a generation; it's time now to study the reason why God gave the prophecies.

We look at our hope in Christ more as an abstract term, and we do not know that our hope in Christ vibrantly lives because of a smallish part of prophecy that tells of what we receive from God for our faith. Hebrews 11:6 says, "But without faith it is impossible to please him: for he that cometh to God must believe that he is, and that he is a rewarder of them that diligently seek him." Paul is saying that there are benefits for those who come to God. Those benefits have been foretold by prophecy. When we have no connection between prophecy and the benefits we will receive, we don't understand how our hope in Christ is established. We don't understand how God is faithful or how God is glorified—all through prophecy. We don't understand that many times in the Bible God shows His great and complete faithfulness by first saying what He will do and then doing it. He tells us it will happen, and then it does. It is then that we lose the connection to our hope in Christ. We run out of gas in our faith and stop being motivated for kingdom service, and then we stop showing up for anything that nurtures our faith.

I'm well aware what 1 Timothy 1:1 says: "Paul, an apostle of Jesus Christ by the commandment of God our Savior, and the Lord Jesus Christ, which is our hope." This verse calls the Lord our hope because the promises are made by Him and are in Him. He has made the promises that tell the future; He is the one who makes the promises come true because He is faithful. Jesus is the one who will ensure that you obtain all you have been promised. So yes, our hope is in the Lord first because He made the promises and He will make them come to pass. Those wonderful promises are rooted deeply in His faithfulness. Of course God is our hope because there is so much more to the Lord God than we could possibly know here on this earth. I think we will need all eternity to learn the riches and depth of who He is.

> God is not a man, that he should lie; neither the son of man, that he should repent: hath he said, and shall he not do it? or hath he spoken, and shall he not make it good? (Num. 23:19)

What motivates you in your faith? We are all aware of the things in our human nature that motivate us to sin, such as lust, hatred, jealousy, revenge, and so on. But what are the things that motivate us to prosper in our faith? What is it about our faith that causes us to do things that are contrary to our human nature and endure a lifetime in faith? It is the Lord Himself and His loving nature and our hope to obtain all the steadfast promises He has given to us that are at our core motivation to be close to Him. Again the promises come from prophecy, words about the future, so a key inspiration for our faith, kingdom service, vision, identity, and evangelism comes from prophecy. A promise made is a hope created. Remember Hebrews 11:6? "He is a rewarder of them that diligently seek Him." Certainly God will reward us for our faith, because like, Sara we judge Him faithful who has promised (Heb. 11:11).

Why Is It There?

Prophecy is an important subject in the Bible, filling over one quarter of all Bible verses, but questions about biblical prophecy have remained for a long time. Questions about prophecy needed to be asked, such as, "Lord, why is there so much prophecy in Your Word? What is Your purpose for it? How did You want it to affect us? Is there a purpose for Bible prophecy today?" Yes! We need to see God's side of prophecy. Did God intend for our generation to have all the doom and gloom of the end times hanging over us? Is that what God intended prophecy to be for this generation? I'll answer that in one word. No! God intended so much more benefit from His words about the future for us.

Most people know that the prophecies about the coming Messiah and the return of Jesus are a central theme to much of prophecy, but there is still more to it than the Messianic and second-coming prophecies. All the books on the end times have colored our perceptions about prophecy for a generation. That is only partly okay. It certainly is a start, but it is not enough. It is not enough because God intended us to know that there so much more to prophecy than the end times. Studying the end times may be the start of a longer journey, with the end of that journey seeing God's love for us and being in relationship with Him.

A book needed to be written to show what the Bible itself says about prophecy. There is a need to understand what God intended prophecy to be. The answers may surprise everyone, especially those who disdain prophecy as it is portrayed today in sermons and books. The answers from the Word of God will provide a better understanding of the much-needed and amazing benefits prophecy gives us right now and an understanding of motivational benefits we will receive when we meet the Lord face to face.

Rethinking Our Thinking

I admit that there is an uphill battle to change how people think about prophecy because the conditioning of the last forty years has taught us to think only one way about prophecy. It will be like swimming against a strong current to convince people who avoid prophecy because of negative experiences with prophecy in their past to change the way they view prophecy. But it is my hope that everyone will see that there is so much more to prophecy than end times, weird doctrine, date setting, or sermons locked in to preaching about current events and the end times.

So change we must, but changing how we view prophecy is hard. Learning multiplication, division, and algebra is hard when all you've known are addition and subtraction. Teachers help children learn math by flash cards and repetition. It helps students learn the new math by constantly pulling up those flash cards: 5 x 5 = 25, 5 x 6 = 30, 5 x 7 = 35, 5 x 8 = 40, 5 x 9 = 45, and so on. I remember that my mom bought some of these flash cards to help me with basic math while I was in elementary school. I needed those flash cards; they helped me to learn the math by repetition. It will be that way in this book too. We will keep the flash cards of repetition coming to remind us what prophecy is, not to redirect but to include it in our thinking with what we have known. It is a way of understanding prophecy that wonderfully supplements everything we have known about prophecy. Having an understanding only about the end times is less than what we should know and experience from the whole picture of prophecy. But knowing about the end times is just the start of a wonderful experience of partnering with the Lord.

CHAPTER 1

The Case for Prophecy

M ention the words *Bible prophecy* in a conversation, and it will induce many responses. There are many differing opinions on prophecy in the church today. There are people who go overboard with it and look for fulfillments in everything. People hate it, people love it. Christians avoid it. Some read it and don't know that what they have read is prophetic, and others learn from it. Some Christians who hear strangers speak about some new doctrine about prophecy imagine the red flags warning of false doctrine are waving vigorously, as though they are about to hear some weird doctrine. From a roll of the eyes in disdain to a magnet for the imbalanced or an argument from a person holding a differing opinion, it is sure to get some response.

There is much opposition to prophecy today, but that is nothing new. There has been opposition to prophecy since ancient times. The apostles had much opposition from false doctrine, some of it within the church, but they still taught about prophecy. The disciples came to Jesus in Matthew 24:3, asking Him, "Tell us, when shall these things be? And what shall be the sign of thy coming, and of the end of the world?" Jesus responded to them at first not by telling them about the end times or about the signs of His coming but by telling His disciples about false Christs, teachers, and deceivers and that many will be deceived. "Take heed that no man deceive you" (Matt. 24:4) was the first thing Jesus said when he responded to their question.

Please take note: the abundance of false teachings does not stop us from teaching. False teaching is opposition from the enemy, and so teaching about the Bible and prophecy must continue because it is truth. We don't stop teaching about the Bible because there is opposition from the enemy. Just be careful of your doctrine, and don't commit to believing in something new you hear until you have matched up what you hear in the rest of the Bible.

Only God Does It

The word *prophecy* in the Greek means to foretell events, to speak under divine influence, or to exercise prophetic office. The study of Bible prophecy is simply the study of what God has said about the future. True prophecy always comes from God Himself, or God may give it to a man called a prophet and that prophet goes and tells it to others. What God has said or that is given in prophecy by a prophet are words about the future. Of course our opinions of what He has said differ widely. Many times in history when the future has been spoken by a prophet, there has been persecution, imprisonment, beatings, and death for the one who spoke the prophecy from God. We are no different today, but today we often just ignore or dispute with the people who talk about Bible prophecy. It is still a difficult subject for many today. Prophecy has had a long and difficult road to understanding what God has said. The wayside is littered with false teaching and false teachers eager to deceive. The only inoculation against false doctrine is to know what is true, and that comes from a good knowledge of the whole Bible. Then with that knowledge we can compare new things we hear with that thorough the filter of the Scriptures.

The heavens declare the glory of God to us every day and night (Ps. 19:1), and like the testimony of the heavens, all Bible prophecy still testifies and still teaches us. It still supplies important essentials for our faith. Jesus came and fulfilled over one hundred prophecies. Even though He fulfilled those prophecies two thousand years ago, they still teach us things about God's faithfulness and power to fulfill His words even though those words might've been spoken centuries before their fulfillment. A part of prophecy's testimony is to tell us that God is almighty, and He can surely make His words about the future come to pass. They testify to all generations that Jesus is faithful to fulfill all the requirements of the law and all the words from God that the prophets spoke. Prophecy is the home of our hope in Christ and exhorts us to live a pure life. Of course there are many more prophecies in the Bible than just the verses on the end times. We need to look at all Bible prophecies and learn why God put so much of it into His Word.

A man after God's own heart said, "Lord, make me to know mine end, and the measure of my days, what it is; that I may know how frail I am" (Ps. 39:4)

The case for understanding Bible prophecy and God's purpose for it in the life of every believer is found in the study of His Word. Every major Bible character has either prophesied or heard prophecy or knew about it. Prophecy has been spoken to individuals, groups, nations, and kings, to Jews and Gentiles. Prophecy foretold of a nation God would work through to show His glory and His purposes to the world. Prophecy foretold of the Messiah, and when Jesus came and fulfilled prophecy those prophecies, they became a solid proof that Jesus was the Messiah. Prophecy gave hope to the people of Israel enslaved in Egypt and inspired Israel to fight its enemies. There are prophecies that have been fulfilled in mere seconds or have taken millennia to bring fulfillment. The sheer volume of prophecy in the Bible demands its study to first see what it says and understand God's purpose for it.

These things alone stand as proof enough to learn about prophecy, but there is much more. Prophecy brings hope, it gives us strength, and it shows God's faithfulness and power as the almighty God. It brings God glory and draws us to faith in Him. Prophecy proves God is alive, and knowing He exists can draw us into relationship and intimacy. All of this comes from prophecy? Yes and even more. It is only through prophecy that we learn about our benefits for faith in God. Only a smallish portion of prophecy tells us about the rewards and inheritance for our faith in Christ. These prophecies are so precious because they are the motivation to purify our lives and faith (1 John 3:3).

Prophecies tell us about our place in heaven with Jesus for eternity, reward for service in Christ, eternal life, resurrection from the dead, and receiving a new body that never feels pain or sorrow and more. But in those scant few verses that tell us about our rewards and inheritance lies the reason that causes us to crucify the flesh (Gal. 5:24), lose our lives for Christ (Matt. 10:39), and spend our lives in service to God as living sacrifices (Rom. 12:1). It is all motivated by our prophetically generated hope in Christ to receive those fantastic benefits.

Help to Do the Opposite

God calls us to do things that are entirely contrary to our human nature. He commands us to crucify the flesh, lose our lives for Christ, and spend our lives in service to others as living sacrifices. God is wise and all knowing. He created not only our bodies but also our minds. He created our emotions. He knows what makes us tick because He designed the things that make us tick. He knows that rewarding us for our service of faith to Him is the way to draw us into the kingdom.

I know living the life of faith has been accused of being boring. I'm sorry, but it is the life that is lived without faith that is boring. It is not dry and dreary service that we perform out of harsh or blind obligation—not in any way. It is a service that is done in joy and excitement, knowing we have an extreme hope beyond the grave. In Matthew 13:43, Jesus said, "Again the kingdom of heaven is like unto a treasure hid in a field; the which when a man hath found, he hideth, and for joy thereof goeth and selleth all that he hath, and buyeth that field." We can easily sell our lives for the treasure God has promised to us. We can do all the stuff that is contrary to our nature because the rewards are so fantastic. It is almost wrong to say that the rewards are so unbelievably wonderful. Hebrews 11:6 says, "But without faith it is impossible to please him: for he that cometh to God must believe that he is, and that he is a rewarder of them that diligently seek him." The list of those rewards for our faith is amazing and includes benefits we receive in this life and in the life to come.

Every Christian ought to be so excited about these benefits. Remember, there is joy even in our salvation (Ps. 51:12). A small portion of Scripture describes the benefits we will receive when we are with the Lord and no longer living by faith. We really have an incredible hope in Christ—so much more than the world has to look forward to—because our hope goes beyond the grave. Peter called the promises of God "exceedingly great and precious" in 2 Peter 1:4. Such great promises produce the strength to deny the flesh and live for Christ. Prophecy helps us to live the life God wants us to live when we know about the promises given through prophecy. Promises given by prophecy strengthen our faith

Doom and Gloom

If you have been neglecting the subject of prophecy in your Bible reading and study, then all of these benefits are good reasons to start studying those things again that give you hope and strength for your faith. Don't settle for anything less than the power that a confident, Christ-based hope brings, but know where that motivating hope comes from.

The end-times prophecies should be popular now for many reasons. Many writers of the current books on prophecy see our generation as the last generation before the Lord returns. If that is true, then yes, the things they write about will happen shortly, and that makes what they write about very important. Showing what this world is about to go through by these books is good because God wants His children to know the future to prepare our hearts for whatever may come. Throughout Bible history

God has placed a vision before many generations by prophecy, and that vision has given hope, warned people, and helped with preparations for what was foretold. Sometimes that vision is a wonderful vision; sometimes it is not so nice. Doom and gloom were present in Joseph's interpretation of Pharaoh's dream about the coming drought and famine. Doom and gloom were hanging over the entire earth in Noah's time, and they were certainly was present in the coming destruction of Jerusalem and the temple hanging over the Jews' heads over twenty-five hundred years ago. Jeremiah's words then included a lot of doom and gloom for the people of Judah.

Of course, prophecy is *not* all about doom and gloom. God intended wonderful benefits to come from prophecy and to be essentials for our faith. Prophecy about our future produces hope. Hope has been an essential part of generations of people both in Bible stories and throughout the world. Knowing the purpose for prophecy has moved many people closer in their relationships with God. Prophecy brings us closer to God, and being close to God is another essential in our faith. God is faithful. Seeing God's faithfulness through His ability to make His words come to pass brings us closer to Him because He is glorified upon prophetic fulfillment.

Think of living in the time of Moses and seeing the words God had spoken to your distant ancestor about spending four hundred years in slavery serving another nation come true in your deliverance. Just imagine seeing the ten plagues of Egypt come to pass exactly as each one was foretold by Moses. Imagine hearing Jesus foretell the destruction of the temple in Jerusalem and still being alive to see it happen, just as He said. Seeing God glorified in this way is essential for our faith. God knows the future; what an amazing thing that is all by itself. What is more amazing is that God wants us to know the future too, and He lets us see it in His Word. However, there is still much more to prophecy than that.

There is no denying that the end times bring doom and gloom into the picture of the future that the Bible presents. I think the horrors that are coming have brought many to faith in Christ. The end-times doctrine is just a tool we may use in our evangelism. The doom of the end times does not have to be an infection that destroys our hope in Christ. It is an affirmation of the faithfulness of God. If our hope is in this world, then yes, it would be something to be feared and dreaded because everything we hoped in would be coming to an end. But our hope is not in this world; our hope is in Christ, and our citizenship is not of this world. I'm not saying that we will be totally insulated from anything that may come, end-times related or not, but we have our eyes on Jesus and not our fears. Fear cancels faith, but a strong hope strengthens every part of our lives in Christ.

If you believe we are living in the end times, then that is just our position in God's timeline for the world. If the people in Jerusalem believed Jeremiah's prophecies about the coming destruction of Jerusalem, then they knew the terrible things that were coming. They would've gone against the popular majority who believed the false prophets who said Judah would defeat Babylon in battle. But they would've known that Judah's sins were too great and punishment was coming to Judah. Once the Jews were in Egypt for a generation, they would've known they were going to be there for a long time serving the Egyptians with hard bondage, according to the prophecy that God gave Abraham two hundred years earlier. That prophecy in Genesis 15:12–16 brought doom and gloom to those living at the beginning of those four hundred years of bondage, but those same words from Genesis were a source of hope toward the end of their enslavement.

Today we are like those enslaved Jews in Egypt who were living in the time at the end of their bondage. Sure, there may be tough things ahead, but we are the redeemed, the heirs of the kingdom, and the apple of God's eye. We live in His protection and grace. God does everything with a purpose, and He has a purpose for putting all the information about the end times into the Bible. It is not for fear, doom, and gloom to negate the faith He wants us to have hope in Him. So again, studying prophecy and studying God's purpose for prophecy is beneficial for us

Three Views

There seems to be three main views and related purposes for prophecy today. First there is the world's view of prophecy, which is filled with all the media-generated stereotypes of crazy, even dangerous people who are into Bible prophecy. We don't have to look very far to see the purpose of those negative images in the media. The purpose for this view is satanically inspired to make the subject of prophecy as weird as possible so it will be ridiculed and so shamed that even Christians won't study it or receive the benefits of knowing prophecy.

Christians who are influenced by this view are not benefiting from prophecy as it was intended, much to Satan's delight. Our spiritual attack alarm bells should be ringing loudly whenever we see this attack on prophecy by Satan. Sadly, it is a very commonplace attack. But we are not sounding any alarm when we see this attack by our enemy; instead, we are shamed away from learning about prophecy.

Second, there is the church's view of prophecy, which for at least the past forty years has focused on the end-times prophecies. The purpose of this view is to warn people, kind of like someone who sees a fire in an occupied building and starts to yell, "Fire!" It is a good view that warns us and causes the church to purify itself. A negative side effect of this view has been the confusion caused by so many views, and that has soured some in the church to loathe hearing anything about prophecy.

Third and most importantly is God's view and purpose for prophecy. His purpose for prophecy is displayed in the Bible; God uses prophecy to reach out to His creation to prove Himself to everyone so that we will move toward Him in faith and trust. You could say that God is reaching out to us just like an evangelist, but prophecy is one of God's tools that He uses to create relationship. His purpose for prophecy is supported by all the benefits He intended for a person who lives the life of faith to receive. A part of God's purpose for prophecy is to exhibit His benefits for us as we live our lives in faith. As His purpose is shown, discussed, taught on, preached on, and understood, the church will enjoy the benefits He intended for us to have. This is the focus the church must relearn today.

The cars we drive have different gears. The transmission has forward, reverse, neutral, as well as lower gears. We use all the gears while driving. Imagine that we ignore the reverse gear and never use it. When we pull into a parking spot or into our garage, we have to put the car into neutral and get pushed out of the parking space so we can put the transmission into drive and go forward. Of course that would be silly; we use our reverse gear all the time while we drive. We want to use all the gears available to us to maximize the benefit of the transmission while driving. If we don't have the use of all our transmission gears, there is something wrong with the car and we fix it.

Our perception of and focus on Bible prophecy needs a bit of direction correction today. We have been studying one small portion of a large picture, and we must step back and see the whole picture. Maybe it is the way in which it is portrayed in books, preached from the pulpit, and taught in Bible classes that needs the refocus. The purpose for prophecy must be written into books, preached from the radio and TV, preached from the pulpit, and taught in Sunday school classes and in Christian retreats. Prophecy today is a doctrine that is sometimes suspended in conflict and in search of a firm foundation to settle it down from the confusion about it that makes some Christians avoid listening to it. I think the disciples of Jesus understood more about prophecy than we do today. They used it often to prove God in their witness to others. The disciples understood the many benefits prophecy holds for everyone.

Over the centuries, we have lost our understanding of prophecy's purpose and have not enjoyed its benefits or used it to reach out to the world. I believe we have been looking at the interpretation and application side of the coin for too long. Direction correction needs to come to the church. It is time to flip that coin over and see prophecy's purpose and many benefits. Once the coin is flipped over, we will have a more balanced view and understanding between God's purpose and the current view of the end times. I believe God has displayed His purpose for Bible prophecy in His Word, and that will become very evident as we go over the Scriptures.

Agreement Is Better

This is a book containing a view about prophecy that we can all agree upon. Understanding God's purpose for prophecy will unify us as a church. It doesn't matter if you think the rapture will happen before, during, or after the great tribulation or if you hold some other view about prophecy. It doesn't matter how much or how little you know about prophecy. The focus herein is God's purpose for it and the ways God wants us to benefit from it. Man didn't put prophecy in the Bible, God did, and He has very specific uses for it. There is a harmony to all prophecy because it originated from the same source. Why would God relate so much of His Word to us that covers the future if He didn't intend for it to benefit us? The things our God does are very amazing and special. He has a plan for all things, and He has a purpose for prophecy too. The one quarter of the Bible that is composed of prophecy has a special purpose for us and our faith. Certainly salvation is what it is because of what Jesus did on the cross; there are so many benefits to salvation.

Once salvation is obtained by repentance and faith, the flow of benefits begins. We are no longer bound by sin and death because Christ has set us free. It is the same way with prophecy; once we understand its purpose, we start to relate to it differently than just trying to understand the interpretations and applications. In a way we look behind the veil of each prophecy and behold God's basis for our hope in Christ and the source of our benefits for our faith.

Prophecy, promises, benefits, prophetic evangelism, our hope in Christ, and our salvation are all inextricably woven together; it's a package deal that starts with God's love for us and desire to be close to us. We understand many things about our faith, redemption, grace, and mercy but not about a subject that floods twenty seven percent of the Bible. We have been avoiding the purpose—indeed, God's purpose—for prophecy for a long time. Maybe the church just forgot about it. We dispute about the things God has written about, and those disagreements cause all the divisions. This is a book that will help show the harmony of prophecy by showing its purpose, God's purpose, which is a central meeting point for all opinions and views to come together. God is love, and prophecy shows God's love for us because prophecy is one of the many ways He reaches out to us to bring us close to Him.

Redoing the Done Deal

Ask Bible-believing Christians today if they believe we are living in the last days, and many would probably answer yes, but ask them to give their reasons to back up that belief and only a few would be able to give more than a few verses of explanation. Is that what prophecy is all about? I think for many Christians, those few prophecies are all that they know. I think we have been trained by all the books and sermons on the end times to sing the same song about prophecy, but we fail to see its astonishing diversity and benefits. It is the trained response; we hear the word *prophecy* and automatically think of the end times.

Today the church thinks there is nothing new to learn about prophecy, no other benefits, and no other way to use or experience it. We need to rethink our belief that response to prophecy equals relationship created. When a bad habit has become the norm, learning the correct way to do something becomes more difficult. First the bad habit has to be unlearned, and then the right way of doing something has to be learned. It is not that learning about something in the Bible, even if it is about the end times, is bad; it is our singular perception that is in need of the fix. It is like a stalled computer waiting for more information to function properly.

Preconditions Undone

I confess—I am guilty of teaching in that pre-conditioned and singular mind-set too. I believed that prophecy was all about the end times, and I never questioned it any further. I now believe that prophecy is much more than that. By prophecy God does something that we can't do—to tell the future so that when we see the fulfillment, we realize that He exists and are drawn to know more about Him in faith and trust. The result is relationship. God filled over a quarter of His Word with prophecy to create and deepen your closeness to Him. Those statements about the nature and purpose of prophecy can only be made that after much study and rethinking of doctrine.

Like wisdom personified in the Proverbs cries out to be listened to and to be understood, God's purpose for prophecy is crying out to be understood so its benefits can be employed and enjoyed by the church today. One of the most important benefits of prophecy is hope. Prophecy creates our hope in Christ. The benefits that are derived from prophecy are many, and they serve to enrich and strengthen our whole Christian experience.

This whole list of benefits is diverse and includes things that we have now and things that we will receive in the future. We have great benefits now, like an unspeakable joy (1 Peter 1:8), a peace that passes understanding (Phil. 4:7), and the indwelling of the Holy Spirit. The things God has promised to give to us are revealed by prophecy and make up a precious inheritance that is stored up for us in heaven. "To an inheritance incorruptible, and undefiled, and that fadeth not away, revealed in heaven you" (1 Peter 1:4). (See also Matt. 6:19–21, 10:42, 16:27, Acts 20:32, Col. 1:5, Rev. 21:7, 22:12.)

The benefits from knowing all Bible prophecy are many, but just a few are: it strengthens our faith, it shows us our new identity, it creates and builds a confident hope, it glorifies God by showing us His complete faithfulness, it builds vision, and it very effectively spreads the gospel. Give prophecy a look, and you will see this subject that takes up a quarter of our Bible has an exceptionally high return value for your study. You have a treasure waiting for you that is wonderfully beyond imagination.

> Know therefore that the Lord thy God, he is God, the faithful God, which keepeth the covenant and mercy with them that love him and keep his commandments to a thousand generations. (Deut. 7:9)

More than Prophecy

This book is much more than a book about prophecy. The title of this book may be *God's Purpose for Bible Prophecy*, but the subject encompasses so much more and permeates through our life of faith. This is a series of three small books about relationship with God and how prophecy transforms itself into promises we place our hope in. They are books about God's complete faithfulness. It is a how-to on evangelism. They are books about God's amazing love for us. Everyone of faith needs the benefits God gives for a life of faith to preserve that precious faith through to the end. God loves us so completely to not only reach out to us but to richly sustain us until that day when we will meet Him face to face.

Often when I mention something about prophecy with someone, I get frowns or that deer in the headlights blank stare and an awkward response that says, "Oh that's nice." It's not that what is being said about prophecy is bad doctrine; it is just that people are unfamiliar with it and don't know what to make of it when they hear it. Often the blank stares mean that their past experience with prophecy has been negative. If it is something they haven't heard before, then they are very wary of it to the point of avoidance. If you are one of those who don't have a clue about that stuff, then this book is for you! This is a primer that will give a foundation on which to build a proper understanding. Understanding God's purpose for prophecy is like learning the ABCs before learning how to write a novel. Many amazing benefits for your faith are waiting for you from your study of prophecy.

I also want this book to be for the person who absolutely disdains the subject of prophecy as it is preached on and written about today. As a part of the group of teachers and preachers on the subject of prophecy, I want to say, please forgive us. Please forgive us for sometimes espousing contradiction that is confusing. Please forgive us for radiating doom and gloom with end-times predictions. Please forgive us for date-prediction failures that put the church in a position of ridicule. You are an audience that may've been offended by some of the extreme proponents of prophecy, and I don't blame you.

I know it is a hard sell to get someone who has a history of abuse from people who spew out falsehood and doom to read an entire book on prophecy. You may be unable to know what to believe because you don't know what to make of all the differing views on prophecy. Please trust that God has filled His Word—including over a quarter of His Word that contains prophecy—with wonders of His love.

Again I say this book will not go into all the interpretation and application of end-times prophecies. I promise I will not try to identify the Antichrist. I will not try to predict dates for the rapture or the second coming of our Lord. I promise I won't try to show all the players in the battle of Armageddon or to talk about a coming one-world government. I assure you this book will be much different than all the rest of the books on prophecy because the aim here is to show God's purpose for all Bible prophecy. God will be glorified for prophecy in this book. I want everyone to experience all the benefits of prophecy as the first-century church did. I'm sure you will be relieved to know that there is so much more to prophecy than showing us about all the doom and gloom about the end times.

This book is also for the person who knows little or nothing about prophecy and is confused by all the differing opinions. This book is also for the seasoned reader of the Bible because it may help you align your view of prophecy more closely with God's purpose for it. God wants His purpose for prophecy to become your purpose for it, and that will cause many people to come to know the Lord and want to serve Him.

I won't say that reading this small series of books will help you sort out all the differing opinions and understand how all the end-times events will play out, but I will say that you will gain a better understanding about prophecy from God's side. If I had a choice between understanding all of the end-times events and precisely how they play out and understanding God's purpose for prophecy, I'd choose the understanding of God's purpose for it in a heartbeat.

I am in awe of God and the way He does things. I am always curious to learn more about Him. I want to see why God put so much about the future into His Word. Things that come from God are not ordinary. The things that come from God are very extraordinary. Gaining some understanding about His nature and how He does things and having our faith benefit as a result is spiritual growth. I believe there will be sights and sounds in heaven that have never been experienced on the earth. God will make that happen. There is an old saying based on John14:1–3 where Jesus says in verse 1, "I go to prepare a place for you." We can see what God created in only six days with the earth the planets and all the creatures He has created. Jesus has been preparing this place for us for the last two thousand years. What can God create in that period of time? It is going to be amazing.

God always does things right; that is why He is righteous. We sin, so I guess you could say that we do things wrong. That is why we are bound by "wrongousness." When God saw our wrongousness, He fixed it in a very special way by sending Jesus to be a perfect sacrifice. God fixed our wrongousness by His righteousness. So now because He fixed our wrongousness, we aren't bound by our past wrongousness. God does things very special. Everything from God is extraordinary, so He must have a wonderful purpose for prophecy too, and I want to know what that is. I want to know experience and enjoy all the benefits God has for me. I want to be open to all God is and wants to do in me.

A Foundation with a Purpose

Maybe I am being too naive to think everyone will agree that this book is a foundational work in our understanding of prophecy, but that is what I believe it is. I should be hearing many sermons on the many benefits an understanding of prophecy brings to the believer, but sadly, I'm hearing mostly silence. The church needs to know this and know it well as a basis for a subject that saturates so much of the Bible. It is my prayer that everyone will get acquainted with it and will have a better understanding of God's purpose for prophecy. I pray that everyone may better enjoy the benefits a good understanding of prophecy imparts and together with that have a closer walk with the Lord. I pray that souls will be won because of its powerful way to evangelize, a way that is readily available for every believer's use. I pray that the Lord's will be done with this book; I give it to Him for His purposes and pray that it will prosper in His hand, according to His will.

Although I have included many scriptural references in this work to help explain things, again I say that this is not a book that will explain all the last-days prophecies in all their proper order and place. It is much more than that. I believe that God has a very specific purpose for prophecy that affects the whole world, and I want to try to show what that is. The Scriptures that are included herein are to show God's purpose for prophecy. Current writers of books on prophecy sometimes miss the work of the Holy Spirit in conjunction with its purpose. I believe that it is the work in our hearts that the Holy Spirit does when we see God prove Himself by bringing His words to fulfillment. That is the reason why prophecy saturates our Bible.

Sometimes Christians only see a small portion or a keyhole view of prophecy's mighty benefits. Not understanding the purpose for prophecy is like living in a large house with some of the rooms closed off. Their doors were shut long ago, and no one ever attempts to go in to find out what is there. Those rooms are beautifully decorated with style and taste, full of wonderful treasures. In the past these rooms were open, used, lived in, and enjoyed, but nowadays not many are even curious about them. The occupants there now just pass by those closed doors with hardly a glance. The riches behind those doors are waiting to be poured out upon their discovery, but sadly the dust gathers and the bounty still waits to be found. I think the purpose and benefits of prophecy are like the treasures in those neglected rooms.

Bible prophecy must be taken out of the fringe elements and brought into the mainstream of Christianity, where it belongs, where it once was long ago, just like all the people in the Bible who experienced its benefits. I want to refute the cultural, social, and even the religious bias against it and make its purpose understandable. I'd like to see every Christian enjoying all the benefits that a good knowledge of it brings into our Christian experience. Once that is done, I think everyone will be more comfortable with prophecy and possibly it will help dry up the sea of people who are into all the weird stuff associated with it.

In Bible times, God's prophets were persecuted for the messages they brought. The words God gave the prophets to say to kings, nations, and people were at times hated, and the prophets were persecuted and killed for saying them. I don't think there is anyone today who would want to kill one of the Bible prophets; instead we look into the word to learn from them. These prophets were righteous people who reckoned that the message they bore was more important than their own lives. We look to emulate their righteous lives more than we look at the messages they were told to speak. Holding the prophets' lives up as examples to follow is necessary, but we must not ignore the messages they spoke that came from the Lord and what happened after those messages were delivered.

Embracing Three Fulfillments

All Bible prophecy falls into three simple categories: fulfilled, unfulfilled, and ongoing fulfillment. The prophecies that are fulfilled are embraced, but those that are yet to be fulfilled, specifically the end-times prophecies, have been at times disdained, misunderstood, and debated by many in the church today. If they are disdained, then they are not taught, and if they are not taught, then they are not understood, and if not understood, then they are forgotten. Then we automatically skip over the portions of Scripture that speak about it as though we are blinded to it. We don't see that a good many familiar and well-known Bible verses are about prophecy. What Christian would acknowledge that he or she intentionally ignores over a quarter of the Bible? No one! But that is what we do when we don't embrace prophecy as much as the other three quarters of the Bible.

Most Christians would say that the prophecies that are yet to be fulfilled are called the end-times prophecies. Well, they are only about half right. Please understand that there is a good portion of Scripture that has yet to be fulfilled that isn't at all about the end times. Yes! It is called heaven, and many Scriptures tell us about what we will receive when we arrive there. End-times Scriptures are about an end of things; heaven is about the beginning of our eternity with the Lord!

Luke 12:37 says, "Blessed are those servants whom the Lord when he comes shall find watching: verily I say unto you, that he shall gird himself, and make them to sit down to meat, and will come forth and serve them." We know that this Scripture is about the faithful servants who are watching when the Lord returns, and they get to partake in the marriage supper of the Lamb as the bride of Christ. Certainly the part about the watching is end-times related, but the rest of this Scripture about the feast with Jesus has no place in the category of the end times Scriptures. Once the authority of this world is taken out and the Lord is reigning, it is the end of the end-times portion of Scripture and the beginning of eternity with Jesus.

Warning, Warning

So many times in the past and into the present people have falsely claimed to be prophets and have their followings. Major cults are usually created by someone claiming to have some prophetic insight. The creation of a cult is often jump-started with someone in a group setting a date for the return of Jesus or claiming some divine revelation exclusively for their own small group. It is no small wonder that those red flags of warning spring up in people's minds whenever they hear about prophecy. The church has had a long and sometimes very negative history with the various effects from people and groups who have espoused a false teaching based in prophecy. Christians have misinterpreted Scripture to the point of quitting jobs, selling what they have, and heading to the mountains because someone in their group claimed the end of the world, the rapture, or Jesus' return was coming on a certain date. The carnal disagreements over Scripture have caused divisions and splits within the church.

It is God who inspires the prophecy; it is man that generates the controversy. But I must say that even with all the controversy, all the writers of the New Testament still kept teaching and writing about it because they saw that its benefits far outweighed the negatives. The subject must be taught carefully in the church today. People who teach on the subject must also be ready to actively engage those who are held captive by false doctrine. Controversy control must be done by those who are knowledgeable in the Word. Confrontations are inevitable, and when done in love and not trying to exert control over people, then it is done the same way any of the apostles or disciples would've done it.

God loves people. He loves everyone, and He even loves the people who espouse false doctrine. Why should we be any less in our love for people? Certainly if someone is trying to preach that false doctrine in your church, he or she must be immediately stopped and given space to be reasoned with and repent. Ushers are sometimes the eyes and ears of the pastor during a service. If an usher overhears someone talking about doctrine to a new believer, then he or she would tell the pastor or elder in the church so that the person who is preaching can be examined in his or her doctrine. If it is false and he or she fails to listen to sound teaching and love, then that person should be shown the door and asked to leave. Every pastor is a shepherd and must protect their flock from false teachings, but all things must be done in love.

Back in the first century, false gods and false religion were long-established institutions, and belief in Jesus was a startup fringe religion. Today the church is institutionalized, and false doctrine is the fringe element. It is because false religion was so well established back then that the first-century believers were well versed in those false doctrines and knew what to do when they were confronted with them. False doctrines were the state religion, and false teachings infiltrated the first-century church. Most if not all the false teachings of today had their roots in the first century. I don't think it would be hard for someone like Paul or Barnabas to confront any false doctrine of today. I think they already had a lot of experience with it in one form or another. Paul was often confronting or correcting some false teaching in the letters he sent to the churches he had visited and preached in during his missionary journeys

Jesus taught many times about prophecy and prophesied often. All of the writers of the books in the New Testament included prophecy in their gospels and letters, and almost all of Revelation's 404 verses are about prophecy. We have entire books of the Bible about some people working in a peculiar occupation who were called prophets. We have divided their works into two categories: Major Prophets and Minor Prophets. They were messengers of God. Their group included people who wrote the books of the Bible, from Isaiah to Malachi, including First and Second Samuel. Paul prophesied and John the apostle wrote the epistles of John and Revelation. Most of the Bible was written by people who were prophets. There is so much prophecy in the Bible, but often we read it and do not even realize we are reading prophetic verses. Trying to read the Bible without reading about prophecy is like trying to go swimming without getting wet.

Moses and Paul on Prophecy

In Numbers 11:29 it says, "And Moses said unto him, enviest thou for my sake? Would God that all the Lord's people were prophets, and that the Lord would put his spirit upon them." In 1 Corinthians 14:5, Paul says, "I would that ye all spake with tongues, but rather that ye prophesied: for greater is he that prophesieth than he that speaketh with tongues, except he interpret, that the church may receive edifying." We look at Moses and Paul as two of the outstanding characters of the Bible, and their opinions matter to us. Moses and Paul wished that all God's people prophesied. Moses and Paul understood the purpose and benefits of prophecy, and they both prophesied. Imagine these two meeting and talking in heaven. One represented the law and one represented a ministry of grace to the Gentiles. I think in their conversation they would agree on all points and still wish that more people prophesied. Why should we feel so differently about prophecy today?

The verses from Numbers and 1 Corinthians show us that it is a fact that Jesus Christ is the same yesterday, today, and forever, as it says in

Hebrews 13:8. The spirit within Moses and Paul showed them the same thing about prophecy. Moses and Paul were separated in time by over fifteen hundred years, but they both felt the same way about prophecy because the same spirit was in them leading them to prophesy. If they were here today, would Moses and Paul be saying the same thing? I think so. Why then do we feel so differently about prophecy today? We shouldn't! There were problems with prophecy then, and there will be problems with it today, but that is not a reason to stop studying it and enjoying its benefits. When the media portrays it negatively, then we should stop and think, "What is behind this attack on something in the Bible that gives so many benefits?" Could it be our enemy wants us to be ignorant of something that adds so much to our life of faith in Jesus?

Imagine your spouse comes home one day and says, "That's it! I'm not driving anymore!" You ask, "What's wrong?" He or she answers, "There are fast drivers and tailgaters, out there so I'm not driving anymore." You would try to convince your spouse that it would be okay to keep driving but to be careful, and you point out that it would be a great inconvenience for your family to stop driving. They say, "No I quit, no more driving for me." It's the same thing with some folks in regard to prophecy. Because of the weird stuff, there are folks who give up on Bible prophecy. Don't give up on Bible prophecy because of the way it is portrayed. Just be careful and enjoy its benefits.

Teaching about God's purpose for prophecy unifies people and helps to eliminate disagreements about its interpretation and application. Differing views about prophecy divided the Jews in their views of where the Messiah came from. Some Jews thought the Messiah would come from Egypt from the prophecy in Hosea 11:1. Some Jews thought the Messiah would come from Nazareth because of the Scripture from Zechariah 6:12 (Nazareth could be interpreted to mean "branch town"). Still other Jews thought that Jesus would come from Bethlehem because of the prophecy from Micah 5:2. Of course these three prophecies were all fulfilled in Jesus, but the three prophecies caused three differing views.

Before Jesus, these differing views were at times hotly debated. One would say, "The Messiah will come from Egypt!" The other would respond, "No, No! He will come from Nazareth." Another would argue, "You are both wrong; the Scriptures clearly say that the Messiah will come from Bethlehem!"

We are no different today because we debate our views about the end times. Seeing only the end-times portion of prophecy divides us into pre-trib, mid-trib, post-trib, and Amillennial positions within the church. We don't learn from the mistakes from the past, and we think our view of prophecy is the right one and other views are obviously wrong. Understanding God's purpose for prophecy unites us with the understanding of its purpose and benefits. It is like standing on the train track while we debate our views, and along comes the locomotive and we have to get off the train tracks to let this powerful train pass. Our end-times pet theories step aside when we know about God's purpose for prophecy. Our much-studied and debated doctrines take a back seat when the purpose is known and understood and the flow of benefits is revealed, released, and enjoyed. I'd much rather supplement my teaching about the end times with God's purpose for prophecy than to teach solely about the end times.

It is common knowledge that much of the Bible is prophetic. Over one quarter of all the verses in your Bible are about prophecy. There are sixty-six books, all 1,239 chapters, and over thirty-one thousand verses in the Bible. If the idea that twenty seven percent of our Bible is about prophecy is even close to accurate, then that means there are over 8,000 verses about prophecy in your Bible. Of course the subject of such a huge volume of Scripture demands our study to see what it says and why it is there. The question of why God related so much of His Word to us in prophecy can be answered in its study. We can't ignore the purpose, power, and benefits of Bible prophecy in the life of everyone God draws into relationship.

23

If you were asked, "What is God's purpose for prophecy?" what would you say? Most people when asked that question would say that it is to reveal the future and to prepare our hearts for what is coming. One writer of a book on prophecy wrote, "Prophecy is history written in advance" [4]. I believe that is a good, solid answer, but it is also true to say that prophecy proves God is God. When we begin to understand God's purpose for prophecy it presents us with a bigger picture of prophecy. Certainly we do prepare our hearts for Jesus' return, but the Scriptures that prophesy about the return of Jesus and the rapture do not cover all the prophecy in the Bible.

It could be said about Bible prophecy that focuses on the end times that we are prepared in our hearts by the things we know are coming. We don't want to miss out on heaven, and knowing the things that are coming purify us so we can partake of eternity with Jesus. That response would be a very legitimate answer for a part of prophecy called eschatology or the "study of the last" (days), but as we are discovering that is not the main purpose for all prophecy.

If you are dismayed to think that prophecy is only about the Antichrist, mark of the beast, one-world government, and Armageddon, then you know by now that I have good news for you. There is so much more to see and to benefit from in Bible prophecy! God's purpose for prophecy is the work that it does in our hearts, and that is the most important purpose of all.

I know many books have been written in the last few decades about prophecy, with so many more written after 9/11. I admit that I have my own ideas about how things will happen, and it will be obvious to the reader that some have leaked out in this work in order to explain its purpose. If you hold a differing view and are offended, I am honestly sorry to offend your view. Please forgive me. I have the same ability of interpretation and application as everyone else who writes on prophecy, but my view of the end times is of absolutely no importance here in this work. The main purpose of this work is to show God's purpose for prophecy. If you are reading with a differing view of the end, then again, I sincerely apologize for any offense. Please keep reading, because if you can overlook some insertions of my views and see the purpose for prophecy, I believe you will be greatly blessed for continuing your reading.

So why does God tell us the future through prophets, dreams, and visions? I believe there is so much prophecy in the Bible because it is for a specific purpose. It has a very important and powerful function for believers and non-believers alike. Let's start first by showing how prophecy works and how this subject permeates through our faith in ways that I believe may surprise many Christians. Understanding God's intended purpose for prophecy has become my basis for understanding all Bible prophecy. It is a view that, after decades of study on the subject, I have only come to understand in the last few years myself.

CHAPTER 2

Prophecy at Work in Well-Known Bible Stories

To demonstrate how much prophecy is a part of the Bible, let's look at some of the most commonly known Bible stories and see how much prophecy was a part of each story. We'll list the prophecies for each story and see how prophecy affected the story. Would we lose some of the best-known Bible stories if it were not for prophecy from God? Let's see! Of course every major character in the Bible heard or was inspired to speak prophecy, so everyone was familiar with prophecy. It was a part of everyday life in both the Old and New Testaments because it was so special. We won't focus on every prophecy every Bible character heard or spoke, only those prophecies that are a part of the most widely known stories.

Adam and Eve

We all know the story of Adam and Eve; they were the first people God created. Did they hear God speak any words about the future? Yes, at least two times. The first is open to interpretation as to whether it is a prophecy. It may be more like a mother saying if you do that, this will happen, but it could be interpreted as a prophecy.

1. Genesis 2:17 says, "But of the tree of the knowledge of good and evil, thou shalt not eat of it: for in the day that thou shalt eatest thereof thou shalt surely die."

2. Genesis 3:15 says, "And I [God] will put enmity between thee [the serpent] and the woman, and between thy seed and her seed; it shall bruise thy head, and thou shalt bruise his heel."

In the first prophecy, God tells Adam not to eat from the Tree of the Knowledge of Good and Evil because if he does, he will die. The prophecy is fulfilled when Adam and Eve eat from that tree and spiritually die. The Lord goes on to tell them the consequences for their disobedience in Genesis 3:16–19. Within the second prophecy God tells them a prophecy that is commonly believed to be the very first Messianic prophecy.

Noah and the Flood

The story of Noah and the great flood has been a well-known story for many centuries. Was there any prophecy in the story of Noah? Of course God told Noah that He was sorry He had created man because violence had filled the earth. God told righteous Noah to build the ark.

1. Genesis 6:7 says, "And the Lord said, I will destroy man whom I have created from the face of the earth; both man, and beast, and the creeping thing, and the fowls of the air; for it repenteth me that I have made them."

2. Genesis 6:13 says, "And God said unto Noah, The end of all flesh is come before me; for the earth is filled with violence through them; and, behold, I will destroy them with the earth. Make thee and ark of gopher wood; rooms shall thou make in the ark, and pitch it within and without with pitch." God goes on to tell Noah instructions for building the ark.

These prophecies are fulfilled in Genesis 8, and some folks may know that God made the rainbows as a token of the covenant between God and Noah (Gen. 9:12–17). It is important to know that without prophecy, mankind would've been wiped out by the flood because Noah and his family would've drowned in the flood. God is faithful and desires relationship with all of us, so He saved Noah and his family.

Abraham and Sarah

We all know of the story of Abraham—how God made a covenant with him and how he and his wife Sarah were childless. It is a well-known story in the Bible. Prophecy was active and at work in Abraham and Sarah's lives too. The first time Abraham heard prophecy was in God's call to him to leave his home in Ur of the Chaldees to a place that the Lord would show him.

1. Genesis 12:1–2 says, "Now the Lord had said unto Abraham, Get thee out of thy country, and from thy kindred, and from thy father's house, unto a land that I will shew thee: And I will make of thee a great nation, and I will bless thee, and make thy name great; and thou shalt be a blessing: And I will bless them that bless thee, and curse him that curse thee: and in thee shall all the families of the earth be blessed."

2. Genesis 12: 7says, "Unto thy seed will I give this land."

3. Genesis 13:16 says, "And I will make thy seed as the dust of the earth: so that if a man can number the dust of the earth then shall thy seed also be numbered."

4. Genesis 17:19 says, "And God said, Sarah thy wife shall bear thee a son indeed, and thou shalt call his name Isaac: and I will establish my covenant with him for an everlasting covenant and with his seed after him."

5. Genesis 17:21 says, "But my covenant will I establish with

Isaac, which Sarah shall bear unto thee at this set time next year."

6. Genesis 18:10 says, "And he said, I will certainly return unto thee according to the time of life; and, lo, Sarah thy wife shall have a son."

Abraham heard many words that God spoke about the future. God made covenants and promised that a son and a great nation would come out of Abraham, all in words about the future. If the prophecies were never spoken, would Abraham's age have affected his ability to have children if he had no hope of having a son? Possibly!

Joseph

We have all heard of the story of Joseph and the coat of many colors his father made for him. We know how Joseph's brothers hated him and sold him into slavery. We've read how Joseph came to be the head of Potiphar's house and how he came to be imprisoned by false accusation. We know that Joseph could interpret dreams, and this gift caused Joseph to be delivered from prison to a position of second in command of the ancient superpower of Egypt. Joseph's ability to interpret prophetic dreams saved Egypt and Joseph's family from certain starvation. Here are the prophecies recorded in Genesis.

1. Genesis 37:5-8 "And Joseph dreamed a dream, and he told it his brethren: and they hated him yet the more. And he said unto them, Hear, I pray you, this dream which I have dreamed: For, behold, we were binding sheaves in the field, and lo, my sheaf arose, and also stood upright; and behold your sheaves stood round about, and made obeisance to my sheaf. And his brethren said to him, Shalt thou indeed reign over us? Or shalt thou indeed have dominion over us? And they hated him yet the more for his dreams, and for his words."

2. Genesis 40:12–13: "And Joseph said unto him, This is the interpretation of it: The three branches are three days: Yet within three days shall Pharaoh lift up thine head, and restore thee unto thy place: and thou shalt deliver Pharaoh's cup into his hand, after the former manner when thou wast his butler."

3. Genesis 40:18: "And Joseph answered and said, This is the interpretation thereof: The three baskets are three days: Yet within three days shall Pharaoh lift up your head from off thee, and shall hang thee on a tree: and the birds shall eat thy flesh from off thee."

4. Genesis 41:25–30, "And Joseph said unto Pharaoh, The dream of Pharaoh is one: God hath shewed Pharaoh what he is about to do. The seven good kine [cows] are seven years; and the seven good ears are seven years: the dream is one. And the seven thin and ill favoured kine that came up after them are seven years; and the seven empty ears blasted with the east wind shall be seven years of famine. This is the thing which I have spoken unto Pharaoh: What God is about to do he sheweth unto Pharaoh. Behold, there come seven years of great plenty throughout all the land of Egypt: and there shall arise after them seven years of famine; and all the plenty shall be forgotten in the land of Egypt; and the famine shall consume the land."

We know that the seven years of plentiful harvests came and went, and Egypt stored much grain against the seven years of drought and famine. Egypt had food only because of Joseph's interpretation of Pharaoh's dream. Of course, the rest of the story is about how Joseph's family came to live in Egypt and eventually become enslaved. No prophecy meant no knowledge of a coming famine, and no food stored and no food to eat in the lean years meant starvation, not only for all of Egypt but also for Joseph and his family.

Moses and Israel's Deliverance

Moses was born in Egypt and grew up and fled to Midian, where he met his wife and had children. God sent him back to Egypt, and he worked with the Lord to deliver the children of Israel out of their oppression and slavery by the Egyptians. Each time there was a plague, there was first a prophecy about the coming plague. We don't need to recount all the prophecies of the plagues; we'll just list the first three and the last of the prophecies of the plagues. You'll see that there was a prophecy before each plague

1. Exodus 3:7–10: "And the Lord said, I have surely seen the affliction of my people which are in Egypt, and have heard their cry by reason of their taskmasters; for I know their sorrows. And I am come down to deliver them out of the hand of the Egyptians, and bring them up out of the land unto a good land and a large, unto a land flowing with milk and honey; unto the place of the Canaanites, and the Hittites, and the Amorites, and the Perizzites, and the Hivites, and the Jebusites. Now therefore, behold the cry of the children of Israel is come unto me: and I have also seen the oppression wherewith the Egyptians oppress them. Come now therefore, and I will send thee unto Pharaoh, thou mayest bring forth my people the children of Israel out of Egypt."

2. Exodus 3:20: "And I will stretch out my hand, and smite Egypt with all my wonders which I will do in the midst thereof: and after that he will let you go."

3. Exodus 7:17: 'Thus saith the Lord, In this thou shalt know that I am the Lord: behold, I will smite with the rod that

is mine hand upon the waters which are in the river, and they shall be turned to blood."

4. Exodus 8:2–3: "And if thou refuse to let them go, behold I will smite all thy borders with frogs: And the river shall bring forth frogs abundantly, which shall go up and come into thine house, and into thy bedchamber, and upon thy bed, and into the house of thy servants, and upon thy people, and into thine ovens, and into thy kneadingtroughs."

5. Exodus 8:16: "And the Lord said unto Moses, Say unto Aaron, stretch out thy rod, and smite the dust of the land that it may become lice throughout all the land of Egypt."

6. Exodus 11:4–5: "And Moses said, Thus saith the Lord, About midnight will I go out into the midst of Egypt: And all the first born in the land of Egypt shall die, from the firstborn of Pharaoh that sitteth upon his throne, even unto the firstborn of the maid-servant that is behind the mill; and all the firstborn of beasts."

Although we didn't list all the plagues of Egypt, it is plain to see that each one started with a prophecy, even if that prophecy was spoken just minutes or hours before it came to be fulfilled. The story of the deliverance of Israel from their bondage in Egypt is also a story about prophecy and fulfillment and the faithfulness of God to do what He says He will do.

The Promised Land

The Promised Land was a fixture in the hearts and minds of the children of Israel during their captivity in Egypt. It was something each one of them knew about. Some of the Jews may've lost hope and scorned the idea of a Promised Land because of their hard bondage. Others had their hope renewed because the time was coming soon for their deliverance from Egypt. But everyone knew it and wondered if it was true or if it was just a story passed down through the generations from Abraham. Here are the prophecies concerning the Promised Land.

1. Genesis 12:7: "And the Lord appeared to Abram, and said, Unto thy seed will I give this land: and there builded he an altar unto the Lord, who appeared unto him."

2. Genesis 13:15: "For all the land which thou seest, to thee will I give it, and to thy seed for ever."

3. Genesis 15:13–14: "And he said unto Abram, Know of a surety that thy seed shall be a stranger in a land that is not theirs, and shall serve them: and they shall afflict them four hundred years; and also that nation, whom they shall serve, will I judge: and afterward shall they come out with great substance."

4. Genesis 17:8: "And I will give unto thee, and to thy seed after thee, the land wherein thou art a stranger, all the land of Canaan, for an everlasting possession; and I will be their God."

5. Genesis 50:24: "And Joseph said unto his brethren, I die: and God will surely visit you, and bring you out of this land unto the land which he sware to Abraham, to Isaac, and to Jacob."

6. Numbers 33:53: "And ye shall dispossess the inhabitants of the land, and dwell therein: for I have given you the land to possess it."

We know that the story of Israel coming into the Promised Land after they came out of Egypt was fulfilled in the book of Joshua. All of the prophecies of the Promised Land were fulfilled. The Jews were only able to call it the Promised Land because the prophecies were promises for their future. All prophecies are future promises. Those future promises are how God shows His faithfulness, and those promises create hope. Two things gave the Jews hope in the midst of their enslavement in Egypt, and both were based on prophecy. The first thing that gave the Jews hope was the prophecies about the Promised Land, and the second thing to give them hope was the prophecy of a time limit to their enslavement. If there had been prophecies about the Promised Land or a time limit to the enslavement, the Jews would have held little hope for their own land and freedom from bondage.

David and Goliath

The story of David and Goliath is one of the best-known stories in the entire Bible. David was the youngest in his family and a sheepherder for his father, Jesse. He came to the battle with food for his brothers and saw Goliath blaspheming the name of God. David soon found himself face to face with this giant of a man. We all know the story. David kills Goliath, and the rest of Israel fights the Philistines and wins a great battle. But before David meets Goliath, something happens with the future king of Israel and the prophet Samuel that brings prophecy into the story.

1. First Samuel 16:13: "Then Samuel took the horn of oil, and anointed him [David] in the midst of his brethren: and the Spirit of the Lord came upon David from that day forward. So Samuel rose up and went to Ramah."

2. First Samuel 17:34–36: "And David said unto Saul, thy servant kept his father's sheep, and there came a lion, and a bear, and took a lamb out of the flock: And I went out after him, and smote him, and delivered it out of his mouth: and when he arose against me, I caught him by his beard, and smote him, and slew him. Thy servant slew both the lion and the bear: and this uncircumcised Philistine shall

be as one of them, seeing he hath defied the armies of the living God."

3. First Samuel 17:45–47: "Then said David to the Philistine, Thou comest to me with a sword, and with a spear, and with a shield: but I come to thee in the name of the Lord of hosts, the God of the armies of Israel, whom thou hast defied. This day will the Lord deliver thee into mine hand; and I will smite thee, and take thine head from thee; and I will give the carcasses of the host of the Philistines this day unto the fowls of the air, and to the wild beasts of the earth; that all the earth may know that there is a God in Israel. And all this assembly shall know that the Lord saveth not with sword and spear: for the battle is the Lord's and he will give you into our hands."

Understand that David was filled with the Spirit of God, and what he said to Goliath that day in the valley of Elah was prophetic. Samuel had anointed David with oil, and the Spirit came upon David before he met Goliath in that valley. What David said to Goliath came true because his words were prophetic. Maybe it was the prophecy that was the motivator that helped David to meet Goliath and win.

The Birth of Jesus

There are many prophecies that Jesus fulfilled when He came to this earth. He fulfilled over one hundred Messianic prophecies while He was here. At Christmastime we celebrate the birth of Jesus by putting up decorations, gift giving, and singing Christmas carols. But there are many prophecies in the Old Testament that speak of Jesus' ancestry, birth, ministry, death, and resurrection. Because the birth of Jesus is so popular, we will look at the prophecies about His birth. Included is Isaiah's well-known prophecy about the virgin birth, but omitted is the before-mentioned prophecy to Adam about the Messiah from Genesis 3:15.

1. Second Samuel 7:12–13: "And when thy days be fulfilled, and thou shalt sleep with thy fathers, I will set up thy seed after thee, which shall proceed out of thy bowels and I will establish his kingdom. He shall build an house for my name, and I will stablish the throne of his kingdom for ever."

2. Micah 5:2: "But thou, Bethlehem Ephratah though thou be little among the thousands of Judah, yet out of thee shall he come forth unto me that is to be ruler in Israel; whose goings forth have been from of old, from everlasting."

3. Isaiah 7:14: "Therefore the Lord himself shall give you assign; Behold a virgin shall conceive, and bear a son, and shall call his name Immanuel."

4. Isaiah 9:6: "For unto us a child is born unto us a son is given: and the government shall be upon his shoulder: and his name shall be called Wonderful Counselor, The mighty God, The everlasting Father, The Prince of Peace."

When Jesus came to the earth, He fulfilled prophecy. When He spoke, He referenced the prophets and even spoke of new prophecies. In these three ways, Jesus was as much a part of the prophetic as He could be. With these and other prophecies about His birth Jesus fulfilled, He proved to be the Messiah, the living God, and our proven Redeemer. Take away these prophecies and others that tell of His coming, and there is nothing to fulfill. Then there is no Messiah to look for, and Jesus would likely not be born because God does nothing without first telling His servants the prophets (Amos 3:7). Jesus' birth was a major way in which God restored us to relationship with Him.

The Crucifixion and Resurrection of Jesus

First we will go over the prophecies of Jesus' crucifixion, and then we will list ones about His resurrection. Listed here are four prophecies from Jesus' crucifixion and another four prophecies about His resurrection.

1. Psalm 34:20: "He keepeth all his bones: not one of them is broken." See also Exodus 12:46 and Numbers 9:12.

2. Isaiah 53:6–7: "All we like sheep have gone astray; we have turned every one to his own way; and the Lord hath laid on him the iniquity of us all. He was oppressed, and he was afflicted, yet he opened not his mouth: he is brought as a lamb to the slaughter, and as a sheep before her shearers is dumb, so he openeth not his mouth."

3. Psalm 22:1: "My God, my God, why hast thou forsaken me? Why art thou so far from helping me, and from the words of my roaring?"

4. Psalm 22:16, 18: "For dogs have compassed me: the assembly of the wicked have inclosed me: they have pierced my hands and my feet. ...They part my garments among them and cast lots upon my vesture."

5. Psalm 16:9–10: "Therefore my heart is glad, and my glory rejoiceth: my flesh shall rest in hope. For thou wilt not leave my soul in hell; neither wilt thou suffer thine Holy One to see corruption."

6. Psalm 31:5: "Into thine hand I commit my spirit: thou hast redeemed me, O Lord God of truth."

7. Isaiah 25:8: "He will swallow up death in victory; and the Lord God will wipe away tears from off all faces; and the rebuke of his people shall he take away from off all the earth: for the Lord hath spoken it."

8. Psalms 68:18: "Thou hast ascended on high, thou hast led captivity captive: thou hast received gifts for men; yea for the rebellious also, that the Lord God might dwell among them."

Jesus lived with and spoke prophecy. He referenced the old prophets often, and He spoke of new things that would come true before He died, of things that would come true before the first century ended, and of things that would come true much, much later. His life was a reflection of the Father, but it was also a fulfillment of many prophecies. He grew up at Nazareth, which is just one hill away from a valley where the final battle of the world will be fought. In a sense, Jesus grew up at Armageddon. He spoke prophecy to the common people He met, to a king, and to the religious rulers of His day. Try as you may, it would be hard to list all the things that Jesus said and not have it saturated with words about the future.

In all these well-known Bible stories, prophecy is very present, and we can see that in some of the stories the story itself would have never happened if it weren't for prophecy. Prophecy is the one common thread of proof throughout the Bible that proves God is real, and once people see that, we come to Him in faith and relationship happens. Certainly the biggest story besides Jesus' ministry and the redemptive nature of His sacrifice and resurrection was the story of the Jews in Egypt. It is a story that covers many chapters, and the reminders that God gave to the children of Israel with were inserted 180 times into their Scriptures over the centuries after they came out of Egypt. Those reminders of Egypt, their deliverance, the desert wanderings, and their entrance into the Promised Land were reminders of what God did in love to nurture His relationship with them.

The popular Bible stories are filled with and sometimes started by prophecy. Of course, there are many stories that are not so well known that are also have prophecy as a prominent feature of the story, so keep reading your Bible and look for those too. I think most Christians would agree that prophecy is a major component of the Bible, and it is worth our time and effort not only to study it and see why it is there but to understand God's purpose for it.

CHAPTER 3
The Four Elements of Prophecy

It is interesting to me how people handle prophecy. Some people get all spiritual and wear robes like people wore in the time of Jesus. They get very eloquent, and sometimes they roll their eyes up and back as if they are going into a trance, fall on the ground, and shake when they are supposedly in communication with God. Their voices get loud, and they try to sound "godly" when they say they are speaking for God. Others try to glorify themselves or mishandle the prophetic, making themselves into an elitist group who are the only ones who know the secret keys to open the mysteries of God in order to gain a position for themselves. Prophecy is a way for some to seize authority and control over others. These things are a perversion of prophecy and its purpose and not anything near what God intended prophecy to be in our lives.

Prophecy is something God wants everyone to understand. Prophecy is easy to understand with just reading and a bit of study. There are no secret keys of wisdom, no secret place, and no secret understanding that you must obtain first to understand it. There is no secret group to join to be a part of so you will understand it. There is no special person to go to and buy these secret keys for a price or to follow who will give you his special wisdom of the ages. I certainly do not want any following or people coming to me and asking for secret or prophetic wisdom or to think I have a special closeness to God above everyone else.

I will tell you right up front that that sort of perverted adoration is nurtured by false prophets and false teachers. Prophecy has a lot of common sense in it. God gave you your common sense to use while reading the Bible. God knows the future, and He tells us about it in His Word. We hear about how God proved Himself again and again, and we see that He really exists and our faith starts. We read His words about the future and learn that God loves us and has promised some pretty amazing things for anyone who has faith in Him. That allows us to draw near to His love and mercy. Pretty simple, isn't it? And it is free to anyone who will just spend some time looking at it.

There are some Scriptures that talk about the mysteries of God, such as Luke 8:10: "Unto you it is given to know the mysteries of the kingdom of God: but to others in parables; that seeing they might not see, and in hearing they might not hear." Ephesians 6:19 says, "And for me, that utterance may be given unto me, that I may open my mouth boldly, to make known the mystery of the gospel." There may be mysteries in the kingdom of God, but they are like open secrets to those who love God and read His Word. They are simply things that are unknown, like the timing of Jesus' return, because no man knows the day or the hour. There are few mysteries to Christians who have faith and read the Word of God.

Prophecy has coherency and reasonableness to it, and I like making it as easy as possible to understand so that as many people as possible will be comfortable with it. There are those who, through their desire for power, have perverted the Word of God. I can say for sure that God does not want only a small group of people to understand His Word and be saved. God wants everyone to come to the knowledge of the truth and be changed by it. John 3:16 displays God's intent for the whole world to be saved: "For God so loved the world, that He gave His only begotten Son, that whosoever believeth in Him should not perish, but have everlasting life." If that verse is true, then why would God reveal His Word to a single small group and those people would be the only ones saved on the whole planet? God makes His Word open and readily available to understand to anyone who seeks after it. It doesn't take college degrees or years of study to understand God's love, salvation, and mercy. All it takes is a heart that loves God to experience it. It's really easy for everyone to understand and partake in it. Mysteries of God are kind of like billboards on the highway. They are there for all who will look at them.

Four Elements

Every prophecy in the Bible has at least four parts or elements to it. The four elements of prophecy are exemplified in the story of the destruction of the temple and the stones being thrown down off the temple mount, as mentioned in the previous chapter. The first element of prophecy is to speak or to hear it. God initiates the prophetic word; He is the source of the prophetic. God Himself spoke the future, like when He spoke to Abraham, or it may be one of the prophets, apostles, or Jesus who spoke the prophecy, such as the temple's demise. It's also possible that someone else, such as Pharaoh or a king, had a dream and a righteous man/prophet interpreted that dream to show the future. We see this happening in the stories of Joseph and Daniel. While he was with His disciples, Jesus foretold of the destruction of the temple in Matthew 24:2, Mark 13:2, and Luke 19:44.

The second element of prophecy is to wait and watch for its fulfillment. In our Bible story about the temple's destruction, this waiting and watching would be the time between when Jesus spoke the prophecy and the temple was destroyed, about thirty-seven years later. The waiting time is centuries, sometimes thousands of years, but it can be very short, such as the prophecy Jesus spoke on the night He was arrested about Peter denying Him three times. That prophecy was probably fulfilled within hours. Sometimes the waiting also has a lot of work involved to prepare for what is coming, such as Noah working to build the ark or the people of Egypt storing grain.

The third element of prophecy is to see it come to be fulfilled. Of course we know that the temple was destroyed in AD 70, perhaps thirty-seven years after Jesus' prophecy. Upon seeing a prophecy fulfilled, we know that it came from God. We know it came from God because we have no ability to know the future. God has just proven Himself to us, and we know that it was God who spoke to us. Is that the end of the matter? Hear it, wait, watch for it, and see it fulfilled—pretty simple, isn't it? For most believers, I think this is where they stop in their understanding of prophecy. Yes, it is cool that God knows the future, and it is amazing when we are able to see the fulfillment of His words. But for most that is where it ends. There is nothing else to understand, and the subject is closed.

There is a fourth element of prophecy that is probably the most important of all the elements of prophecy, and it helps us on our way to understanding the true purpose of biblical prophecy. The fourth element of prophecy goes one step beyond prophetic fulfillment. It is in the fourth element that we understand God's purpose for prophecy. The function of the first three elements of prophecy is to induce the fourth element. The fourth element of prophecy goes into our hearts. It is the most important because of what happens inside us when we know that a prophecy has come to pass.

When prophetic fulfillment, comes we have many reactions. Some people doubt the prophetic fulfillment, some folks scorn and ridicule it, and some decide to have faith because they believe God has proven His existence by it. This is the intended and desired reaction to any fulfillment, and this is when the fourth element of prophecy happens. It is the work in our hearts that makes the last element of prophecy so important. The fourth element of prophecy may be the reason why God filled so much of His Word with it. When we hear God's words spoken in prophecy, there is some wondering to see if it will come to be fulfilled. When we see the fulfillment, we realize He is real and that He has just proven Himself to us. Then we recognize that He is an almighty God working in ways we cannot see to bring His words to pass. When we realize all this, we are drawn to God in faith and trust, resulting in relationship. Of course this is the purpose for prophecy—the relationship with God that it creates.

The External and the Internal

Thanks be to God, He made the fourth element of prophecy to work inside of us, in our minds and hearts. When we talk about the common and widely held views of the end times, we talk so much about the external things of prophecy, like the timing of the rapture (pre-trib, mid-trib, post-trib), the mark of the beast, and Armageddon. We debate about whether the abomination has already happened or if it is a future event. We talk about the predicted natural disasters and so on, but all these things and events are external things. The purpose of prophetic fulfillment is meant to work on us from the inside out. The fourth element of prophecy—the work in our hearts—was meant to work hand in hand with the events. It is the work that the fourth element does inside us with the Holy Spirit to tug on our hearts and minds to pull us in closer and closer to the Lord.

The reason why prophecy exists is to provide a proving ground of events that reach into our hearts with proof of God's existence so we will fully turn to God in faith. Prophecy was meant to do that. When the church's view of prophecy includes only events about the end times, it is mostly about the external things. The events are like a cream that you put on the surface of your skin; it is a topical ointment, used externally only. The fourth element is taken internally like a pill that you swallow, and it works on the inside. Prophecy was meant to affect us in so many ways; its effect is systemic, with salvation, hope and ministry, with outreach, identity, eternity, and all of our experience in our lives with Christ.

Once we have come to the Lord and are in relationship with Him, then the purpose of prophecy changes gears, if you will, to fill us up with hope to strengthen us. By now you can see that hope is one of the most essential ingredients in our faith, but remember this is a hope like no other hope on earth. This is a hope born out of the prophecy/promises of God. Our hope in Christ is special. It has been designed by God to help us to be with Him for eternity, and it is ours until we meet Jesus face to face. Do you understand that this is the good work that God is doing in you? This is the good work Philippians 1:6 describes: "Being confident of this very thing, that he which has begun a good work in you will perform it until the day of the Lord Jesus Christ." The good work God keeps performing until we all meet Jesus is to keep being faithful to His spoken word to give us hope that enables us to persevere on our faith

The original purpose still works in us to keep proving the Lord to remind us of His love for us by showing His absolute faithfulness. By His faithfulness, He shows us His ability to give us what He has promised to us and that greatly assures that we will receive our inheritance in Christ.

Prophecy shows us God's heart for people by the multitude of things He does, including the quarter of the Bible containing prophecy that was written to draw us to Him. It is about creating the closeness in our relationship with our loving Lord and feeling completely loved by Him. Sure, prophecy is about the events, but once we learn about the events and gain an understanding, we then go internal with what God has done to experience the wonderful purpose; it's the place where we dwell with God. For a long time, the church has been external with the events. Now it is time to take it internally so its purpose for it can be fulfilled, experienced, lived in, empowered by a confident hope, and brought forth to a new generation.

Ten thousand years from now, all the events about the end times won't matter much, but the relationships with the Lord that prophecy created will be everything. Ten thousand years from now, there will be people who will be in heaven with the Lord because of their heart's response to God when He proved Himself to them by prophecy and when they recognized that prophecy proved God's existence. The prophecies served to bring us to the place where relationship could start and strengthen us to live the rest of our lives in obedient faith right on into eternity. The use of prophecy is one of God's kingdom builders.

CHAPTER 4
The Prophecy of Jonah

Jonah is called one of the Minor Prophets. The whole book of Jonah is only four chapters long, but what happened in those four chapters makes the book of Jonah stand tall among all the books of the Bible. This book of Jonah is of major importance not only for what happened for the people of Nineveh, but it also shows God's love for a Gentile city outside of Israel. It is one of the greatest examples in the Bible of how God desires for everyone to respond to prophecy.

The time frame Jonah prophesied was after the prophet Elisha and before the ministries of the prophets Hosea, Amos, Micah, and Isaiah. The story of Jonah is one of the most popular stories in the Bible. Every Sunday school child has heard the story of how Jonah fled from the Lord, was thrown overboard from a ship, and was swallowed by a great fish, but as we will soon see, the story of Jonah is much more than the prophet being swallowed by a fish.

Nineveh's History

To emphasize the importance and standing of the book of Jonah, here is a little background on Nineveh and the historical setting of the book of Jonah. Nineveh is first mentioned in the Bible in Genesis 10:11, where Asshur went out to build Nineveh, but the text may actually be talking about the idolatrous Nimrod building the city of Nineveh. It was a huge and very evil ancient city. Nineveh had more than one hundred and twenty thousand residents (Jonah 4:11) living there at the time of Jonah's prophecy. The text may be indicating that the population may've been much higher than one hundred and twenty thousand and could've been as high as six hundred thousand.

Nineveh worshipped false gods and built temples to at least six of their false gods. Nineveh was a religious center and a destination for those who worshipped these man-made false gods. Because Nineveh was a religious destination for the worshippers of false gods, the population of the city probably swelled with worshippers of false gods, especially if there was a celebration honoring some false god at the time of Jonah's visit.

The story of Jonah probably took place about 800 to 750 years before Christ. Jonah's name appears in 2 Kings 14:25 as being a prophet and a resident of Gath-Hepher, a small village about three miles northeast of the town of Nazareth. That reference from 2 Kings meant that Jonah lived during the reign of King Jeroboam in Israel and King Uzziah in Judah in the days of the divided kingdom.

Archeologists have discovered the ancient ruins of Nineveh in northern Iraq across the Tigris River from the present-day Iraqi town of Mosul. The capitol of Assyria, Nineveh was the oldest and biggest city in the Assyrian empire. Assyria had been a power in the earlier 800s BC and struggled as a power in the time of Jonah, but historically Assyria was both an enemy and a terror to Israel. It was later, after the story of Jonah, that King Sargon II in 722 BC carried away the people of the northern kingdom of Israel into exile. It was King Sennacherib who even later in 701 BC made war against Judah and Jerusalem. It was still later in 612 BC that Nineveh was destroyed as predicted by the prophet Nahum. Later generations of Assyrians fell back into the same sin that brought Jonah to Nineveh, but they were destroyed because they didn't heed the prophecies of Nahum, another prophet God had sent to them.

Jonah probably wanted revenge against Assyria as an enemy of Israel and as idol worshippers as the basis of his refusal to go and prophesy in Assyria. He wanted the Gentile enemy of Israel to be destroyed and not forgiven. His emotions got in the way of God's plan for Nineveh.

Repentance from the Fish

The story starts with the word of the Lord coming to Jonah in the very first verse of the book. In the second verse, the Lord told Jonah to go to Nineveh and "cry against it." In other words, God told Jonah to prophesy against Nineveh. Jonah wanted to see Nineveh punished for their great sin. Somehow Jonah knew that if he went to Nineveh and gave the word from the Lord, the Ninevites would repent and the Lord would forgive them and not punish them.

Jonah fled from the Lord and got on a boat to Tarshish. A fierce wind came, and the men aboard the boat were very afraid that the boat would sink. The men on the boat knew that Jonah was fleeing from the presence of the Lord. They cast lots to find out who was responsible for this great storm, and the lot fell upon Jonah. The men asked Jonah what they should do, and Jonah said to them that they should throw him overboard into the sea. They didn't want to do that and instead tried to row all the harder, but the storm was against them very fiercely. They had no choice, and according to Jonah's own word, they threw Jonah overboard lest some innocent blood was shed because of Jonah.

God had prepared a great fish, and it swallowed up Jonah. Jonah cried out to the Lord from the belly of the fish. God heard Jonah's cry of praise and repentance and spoke to the fish, and it vomited Jonah out upon dry land. Imagine people swimming and laying on the beach and this huge fish comes up to the shore and vomits a man out of its mouth. Jonah probably didn't smell too nice. God told Jonah again to go to Nineveh and preach to it. Jonah obeyed and went to Nineveh.

"So Jonah arose, and went unto Nineveh, according to the word of the

Lord, Now Nineveh was an exceeding great city of three days journey" (Jonah 3:3). This reference doesn't mean that it would take Jonah three days to get to Nineveh; it means that Nineveh was a three-day journey to go around the outside of the city, or it could mean it was a three-day journey to go through the city. Either way, Nineveh was a huge city. If Jonah received the prophecy in his hometown, he would've had to walk about five hundred miles to Nineveh, even further if He was on the Mediterranean Sea coast after coming out of the fish. It was not an easy trip in those days.

Prophecy Causes Repentance

The prophet entered the city, went a day's journey into the city, and said, "Yet forty days and Nineveh shall be overthrown." Jonah uttered these eight words, and that was enough for the people of Nineveh to repent. Jonah 3:5 says, "So the people of Nineveh believed God, and proclaimed a fast, and put on sackcloth from the greatest of them to the least of them." The king even had all the animals covered in sackcloth. Verse 3:8 says, "But let man and beast be covered with sackcloth, and cry mightily unto God: yea, let them turn every one from his evil way, and from the violence that is in their hands." In 3:10 it says, "And the Lord saw their works; that they turned from their evil way; and God repented of the evil that he said that he would do unto them; and he did it not."

Remember that Nineveh was a city of three-day journey (Jonah 3:4). Jonah got only one day's journey through the city proclaiming the message. It may be that Jonah was proclaiming the word of the Lord while on his way through the city and that his word spread so fast that it reached the king, and immediately upon hearing the word of Jonah, the king proclaimed the fast with sackcloth and ashes. Jonah didn't have to go all the way through the whole city proclaiming the word of the Lord; he got only one day's journey through it, and the people spread the word faster than Jonah could walk.

I know that we focus a lot on Jonah's anger and refusal to obey God and the great fish swallowing him up; we popularize it into a common children's story, but that is not in any way the heart of its story. The story of Jonah isn't about Jonah or the great fish; it is about a relationship God started with an entire city through prophecy. Please understand that a prophecy started repentance, and that is the first step beginning a relationship with God. The Lord wants us to know Him with intimacy. The Lord wants us to be close with Him. Prophecy is a part of God's evangelism to the whole world. The prophetic testimonies of God are another part of God's outreach to the people of the world. God reached out to the people of Nineveh by prophecy to create relationship with all the people of that city. Imagine saying eight words and having at least one hundred and twenty thousand people get saved, but remember they got saved by the words God gave Jonah to say.

The prophecy alone was enough to make the people of Nineveh repent. The king and the people hastened to repentance; after all, they only had forty days before the prophecy would come true and the city would be overthrown. They didn't want to see the fulfillment of the prophecy that would've likely brought destruction and death. God reached out to the people of Nineveh by a time-stamped prophecy of their destruction. Nineveh would expire in forty days. God's grace for Nineveh was manifested in sending Jonah. Sometimes prophecy without fulfillment touches hearts and causes repentance, forgiveness, and relationship.

In the story of Jonah, all four elements of prophecy were not needed to start relationship with the Lord. The Ninevites were put into a very short waiting and watching period upon hearing the word of Jonah because the prophecy had a date stamp of forty days. The people had to act quickly. The folks in Nineveh skipped over the third element of prophecy, which is seeing the fulfillment; they went right into repentance and relationship. They experienced three of the four elements present, and that was enough to bring the people of Nineveh into relationship with God. They heard the prophecy, and they knew it was true; they repented and started relationship with God. The folks in Nineveh repented immediately.

All four elements of prophecy are not needed today when the end times prophecies are so popular. People who are into the end-times prophecies know that many of those prophecies haven't been fulfilled, yet there is anticipation to those prophecies stirring in our hearts today to purify our lives before God, knowing that the time may well be very close for the Lord's return. Therefore there are many positive reactions to prophecy where all four of the elements of prophecy do not need to be present to fulfill God's purpose for prophecy.

Second Peter 3:9 says, "The Lord is not slack concerning his promise, as some men count slackness; but is longsuffering to us-ward, not willing that any should perish, but that all should come to repentance." God wanted the people of Nineveh to repent. God was very willing to stop the coming punishment for the people of Nineveh upon their sincere repentance. The story of Jonah is one of the greatest stories of prophecy because those wicked people reacted exactly the way God wants all people to react when they experience prophecy. The people of Nineveh didn't need to see fulfillment of the prophecy that Jonah bore to that city; they knew that they would be judged in forty days. God's grace for the evil city of Nineveh had an expiration date.

Of course, with fulfillment comes proof of God's existence. If God exhibits His existence by prophetic fulfillment, then the reaction to that fulfillment is to follow Him. The people of Nineveh didn't want prophetic fulfillment. Because of the way they reacted, I'd say that the Lord was known by the people of Nineveh, or at least they knew of the Lord because of their reaction to Jonah's prophecy. How would they know to react with repentance and sackcloth and ashes? That was a mostly Jewish reaction in repentance with God. There are many examples of repentance with sackcloth and ashes in the Old Testament, and Jesus mentions repentance with sackcloth and ashes in Matthew 11:21.

Nineveh was over five hundred miles away from Jerusalem, and still they knew of the Lord in Nineveh. Most people in that time would've known about the Lord's dealings with the Jews starting in the time of Abraham. They would be familiar with the story of Jewish enslavement in Egypt and their deliverance. The people of Nineveh would've heard the stories of King David and Solomon and the temple of God. Their repentance with sackcloth and ashes showed they were familiar with the Jewish religion. They knew Jonah was Jewish and he was speaking the words of the true God. The people of Nineveh left their faith in their false gods and embraced the true God.

With this particular prophecy, the people of Nineveh didn't need or want to see the proof of prophetic fulfillment to repent. Their great repentance was enough for the Lord to stop the coming judgment because obedience and relationship follows true repentance. They started a relationship with the living God. This is God's purpose for all prophecy—to create and deepen relationship with everyone. By prophecy God does something that we can't do—that is to tell the future so that when we see the fulfillment, we realize that He exists and we are drawn to know more about Him in faith and trust and the result is relationship.

CHAPTER 5

The Woman at the Well

Prophecy changes hearts and causes faith. The supernatural from God causes us to rethink what is real, who we are, and who we are following. We are thinking of what God has said, and it causes us to doubt our own direction in life. When we hear prophecy and know it is from God, we are drawn to Him in faith and trust and that starts a relationship with the Lord that grows into intimacy. There are many stories in the Bible where a prophecy jumpstarted soul searching, repentance, and relationship with God.

Talking about Spiritual Things

The story of the Samaritan woman who met Jesus at the well is in John's gospel in chapter 4 and is a well-known Bible story.

> Then he cometh he to a city of Samaria which is called Sychar, near to a parcel of ground that Jacob gave to his son Joseph. Now Jacob's well was there. Jesus therefore, being weary with his journey, sat thus on the well: and it was about the sixth hour. There cometh a woman of Samaria to draw water; Jesus saith unto her, Give me to drink. (For his disciples were gone away unto the city to buy meat.) Then saith the woman of Samaria unto him, how is it that thou being a Jew, asketh drink of me which am a woman of Samaria? For the Jews have no dealings with the Samaritans. Jesus answered

and said unto her, I thou knewest the gift of God, and who it is that saith to thee, Give me to drink; thou wouldest have asked of him, and he would have given thee living water. The woman saith unto him, Sir thou hast nothing to draw with and the well is deep; from whence then hast thou that living water? Art thou greater than our father Jacob which gave us the well, and drank thereof himself, and his children and his cattle? Jesus saith unto her, Go call thy husband, and come hither. The woman answered and said I have no husband. Jesus said unto her, Thou hast well said, I have no husband: For thou hast had five husbands and he whom thou now hast is not thy husband: In that sadist thou truly. The woman saith unto him, Sir I perceive that thou art a prophet. Our fathers worshipped in this mountain: and ye say, that in Jerusalem is the place where men ought to worship. Jesus saith unto her, Woman, believe me, the hour cometh, when ye shall neither in this mountain, nor yet at Jerusalem, worship the Father. Ye worship ye know not what; we know what we worship: for salvation is of the Jews. But the hour cometh, and now is, when the true worshippers shall worship the Father in spirit and in truth: for the Father seeketh such to worship him. God is a spirit and they that worship him must worship him in sprit and in truth. The woman saith unto him, I know that Messias cometh, which will tell us all things. Jesus saith unto her, I that speak unto thee am he. And upon this came his disciples, and marveled that he talked with the woman: yet no man said what seekest thou? Or Why talkest thou with her? The woman then left her waterpot, and went her way into the city, and saith to the men, Come see a man, which told me all things that I ever did: is no this the Christ? Then they went out of the city, and came unto him.

Skipping down to John 4:39, this story continues:

> And many of the Samaritans of that city believed on him for the saying of the woman, which testified, He told me all that I ever did. So when the Samaritans were come unto him, they besought him that he would tarry with them: and he abode there two days. And many more believed because of his own word; And said unto the woman, Now we believe, not because of thy saying: for we have heard him ourselves, and know that this is indeed the Christ, the Saviour of the world.

Jesus was weary from his travels, and He was without His disciples, who had gone into a town to buy food. Jesus was resting beside a well outside a Samaritan town. Along came the Samaritan woman, and Jesus asked her for a drink. The woman responded scornfully, "How is it that thou, being a Jew, asketh drink of me, which am a woman of Samaria? For the Jews have no dealings with the Samaritans." Jesus answered her according to spiritual things. He said, "If thou knewest the gift of God and who it is that saith unto thee, Give me to drink, thou wouldest have asked of him, and he would have given thee living water."

She ridiculed Him and said, "Sir thou hast nothing to draw with, and the well is deep: from whence then hast thou that living water? Art thou greater than our father Jacob, which gave us the well, and drank thereof himself, and his children and his cattle?" Jesus continued to answer her according to spiritual things by saying, "Whosoever drinketh of this water shall thirst again: But whosoever drinketh of the water that I shall give him shall be in him a well of water springing up into everlasting life."

Jesus started to reveal the woman's past to her even though He had never met her. He started to use prophecy to reach out to this woman, who initially disdained Him. In verse 21 He prophesied to her.

> Jesus saith unto her, Woman believe me, the hour cometh, when ye shall neither in this mountain, nor yet at Jerusalem,

worship the Father. Ye worship ye know not what: we know what we worship: for salvation is of the Jews. But the hour cometh and now is when the true worshippers shall worship the Father in spirit and in truth: for the Father seeketh such to worship him.

After He revealed that He knew her past and spoke prophetic things to her, this woman's cold heart melted. "The woman saith unto him, I know that Messiah cometh, which is called the Christ: when he is come he will tell us all things. Jesus saith unto her, I that speak unto thee am he" (John 4:25). Now she was asking sincere questions of Jesus. Her attitude had completely changed. Jesus spoke revealing and prophetic words to the Samaritan woman, and those words opened up her interaction and her heart. The woman left, went into her city, and told everyone about Jesus. The city of the Samaritan woman came out to hear Jesus. Verse 41 says, "And many more believed because of his own word." Jesus used the Samaritan woman as a point of faith to bring out her town to meet Jesus and be saved. Jesus talked about prophecy with the Samaritan woman, and that helped to produce faith in that city of the Samaritans. Whenever Jesus spoke, He included a lot of prophecy in His words. It was the spark that led many in that city of the Samaritans to believe on Jesus as their Messiah.

As in the story of Jonah, this story of the Samaritan woman and the people of her city didn't need to wait for the fulfillment of Jesus' prophetic words to start relationship with God. Of course, like the Jews, the people of Samaria knew prophecy and were looking for the Messianic prophecies to be fulfilled. When Jesus came to that city, they saw fulfillment and started relationship with the Lord.

CHAPTER 6
Remember Egypt

Everyone knows the story of how Israel became enslaved in Egypt. The Bible story of the Jews in Egypt is a long one compared to other stories in the Bible. It starts in Genesis chapter 37, where Joseph's eleven brothers hate him and sell Joseph into slavery, and the story ends twenty-four chapters later when the nation of Israel leaves Egypt in Exodus 12. Of course, the story doesn't end there; the story continues through the books of Exodus and Joshua, into the desert, and on to the Promised Land. It is a huge story of millions of people delivered out of bondage and into freedom to possess a land chosen for them by God. The whole story started with a prophecy to Abraham in the fifteenth chapter of Genesis two hundred years before the family of Israel went into Egypt. God told Abraham in Genesis 15:13–14,

> And he said unto Abram, Know of a surety that thy seed shall be a stranger in a land that is not theirs, and shall serve them; and they shall afflict them four hundred years; And also that nation, whom they shall serve, will I judge: and afterward shall they come out with great substance.

One of the reasons the Jews in Egypt looked for a Promised Land is in a following verse, Genesis 15:18, "In the same day the Lord made a covenant with Abram, saying, 'Unto thy seed have I given this land, from the river of Egypt unto the great river, the river Euphrates.'" Chapter 15 continues on to describe the boundaries of the Promised Land.

A second time God foretold of the land by prophecy in Genesis 26:2 when God appeared to Isaac.

> And the Lord appeared unto him, and said, go not down into Egypt; dwell in the land which I shall tell thee of: Sojourn in this land, and I will be with thee and unto thy seed, I will give all these countries, and I will perform the oath which I sware unto Abraham thy father; And I will make thy seed to multiply as the stars of heaven, and will give unto thy seed all these countries; and in thy seed shall all the nations of the earth be blessed.

Again in Genesis 50:24 we find a prophecy concerning Israel coming out of Egypt by Joseph when he was 110 years old. "And Joseph said unto his brethren, I die: and God will surely visit you, and bring you out of this land unto the land which he sware to Abraham, to Isaac, and to Jacob." Notice that all three of the times the land is mentioned in the three references that are in the future that the children of Israel will receive the land. It is only by prophecy that the children looked forward to a land of their own that was promised to them by God while they were still slaves in Egypt.

God renamed Abram "Abraham" (meaning: father of a multitude), and Abraham was Jacob's grandfather. Of course God also renamed Jacob "Israel" (Hebrew: *Yisrael*, which means "saved by" or "striven with God"). Jacob/Israel was the one who had twelve sons, and the descendants of these twelve sons became the basis for calling them the twelve tribes of Israel. Of course Jacob/Israel's twelve sons became known both as the twelve tribes of Israel and the children of Israel. There were other details in the makeup of the twelve tribes, but we will leave it this way for simplicity.

Jacob moved with his sons and their wives to Egypt, knowing fully what God had told his grandfather Abraham. He didn't have to wonder if the land his family was moving to was the land God told his grandfather about. Genesis 46:3 says, "And he said, I am God, the God of thy father: fear not to go down into Egypt; for I will there make of thee a great nation. I will go down with thee into Egypt; and I will also surely bring thee up again: and Joseph shall put his hand upon thine eyes." There is no mention here about Egypt being the land where they would be afflicted for four hundred years.

Reminders of Love

Let's say that you do something for your son or daughter that requires a lot of effort and takes a long time to do. What you do is hard, and you work at it faithfully until it is done. The beneficiary of all this work you do is only your child. After it is done, you may remind the child from time to time what you did for him, especially if he is unappreciative of what you did. Reminding him of what you did is a natural thing to do to prove how much you love him. Each time you remind the child, he rolls his eyes in disdain. But you keep reminding him anyway. Your reminders are not meant to nag but to prove how much you love him. Your hope in the reminding is that he will respond in kind to your love. The things you did for him have no effect on him, and he even does things that are against you and all that you did for him. He comes to be involved with someone else, and he gives that person all the credit for what you did and are thankful to someone else for all you did for him.

After Israel came out of Egypt, they worshipped other gods and gave their false gods credit for their deliverance after God did so much to free them from the slavery of Egypt. One of the main testimonies of God in the Bible was that He delivered Israel out of Egypt. This is the biggest thing God did to prove Himself to the Jews, who benefited from their deliverance from slavery in Egypt. The result of all that God did was to have His children go and serve other gods.

Thanks and praise is to God that He is not like us. He demonstrates His love for us through His longsuffering with us. He is patient and loving and willing that none should perish. He reminds us of His great love for us and of all that He has done for us. He gave us His word so that we can learn about the things that He has done so that we can learn how to follow Him and be close to Him.

The Bible contains so much prophecy, but it is also a book of reminders— these reminders are about what God did for the Jews. Reminders of how God kept His Word to show His faithfulness. They are reminders of how they were delivered from Egypt, bondage, into freedom and into a land that God gave them. God says the word by prophecy, and then He keeps His prophetic word to all generations, and that shows His complete faithfulness. God reminds the Jews of many aspects of their Egyptian enslavement. The Lord reminds them of His faithfulness in their relationship. The Bible records 180 of these reminders throughout the rest of the Bible after they came out of Egypt.

We also see this keeping of the prophetic word in the over one hundred prophecies concerning the Messiah, which Jesus fulfilled almost two thousand years ago. The story of the Jews in Egypt started by prophecy, and their coming out of Egypt fulfilled prophecy. Each one of the ten plagues of Egypt was first foretold by prophecy. The Jews were helped in their deliverance from Egypt by prophecy. God created vision in the Jews while they were in hard bondage in Egypt by prophecy.

Remember Proverbs 29:18, "Where there is no vision, the people perish." Without the vision of the Promised Land that the prophecies provided the Jews and without the part of the prophecy that gave a time limit to their enslavement in Egypt, the Jews would probably still be in Egypt serving the Egyptians. But it was those prophecies God spoke to Abraham and Joseph that gave vision. The Jews did come out and go to the Promised Land, just as the prophecies foretold. God made it happen just as He said, and that shows so many great things about Him. "My covenant will I not break, nor alter the thing that is gone out of my lips" (Ps. 89:34).

Birth of a Nation

You could say that God used Egypt as a harsh surrogate to give birth the nation of Israel when they came out of Egypt. The harshness of Egypt made it so that no one wanted to stay in Egypt, and the children of Israel wanted to come out and go to the Promised Land. They were a family when they went into Egypt, when they left there they were a nation. They left their home in Canaan to go into Egypt numbering sixty-six people (Gen. 46:26); counting Joseph's family already in Egypt, they numbered seventy people. They grew to six hundred thousand men (Ex. 12:37), not including women and children who came out of Egypt. God uses Egypt as a birth mother for His chosen nation, and He guides that new baby home to the Promised Land.

I have heard Bible teachers estimate that as many as one to two million people may have come out of Egypt. It is entirely possible that their number may've been much higher. "And the children of Israel were fruitful, and increased abundantly, and multiplied, and waxed exceeding mighty, and the land was filled with them" (Ex. 1:7). Remember, Israel was fruitful because God blessed them to have large families. Large families were very desirable in that time and culture because the more children you had, the more workers you had to tend a family business. But Israel had something that no other people had at that time—God's blessing upon them to make them fruitful. Because of their fruitfulness, they easily could've numbered over five or six million, counting the women and children when they left Egypt.

God constantly reminded the nation of Israel of what He did to show them how much God loves them and to show that they are in covenant relationship with the almighty God. The testimonies of God are about His love, His greatness, His longsuffering, and what He has done to keep His word. All these reminders also are a part of the testimonies of God. Just like the story of Jewish bondage in Egypt, it is in the testimonies of God that we find His desire to be close with everyone.

Joseph came into power in Egypt because God was with him, and God gave Joseph the gift of interpreting prophetic dreams. That gift of interpretation of prophetic dreams caused Pharaoh to give Joseph rule in Egypt second to only Pharaoh himself. The way Israel came to be in Egypt was because of agricultural reasons because there was no rain. The lack of rain produced a severe drought, so there were no crops; no crops meant no food, and starvation would soon follow, so the sons of Jacob went to Egypt to buy grain to avoid death by starvation.

Joseph was unaware of God's ordained mission for his life. He eventually came to realize that he was in Egypt to help his family, but going to Egypt also meant the beginning of their four hundred–year enslavement. A pharaoh came to power thirty years later who that didn't know Joseph or his brethren. The new pharaoh became suspicious and afraid of the growing numbers of the children of Israel, and he enslaved them lest the Hebrews help their enemies to fight against Egypt. In just thirty years, this seventy-member family grew so much that it made the Egyptians feel threatened for the security of their nation. Now that is a fruitful family! The prophecy God gave to Abraham was partly fulfilled here. The rest of the prophecy that God gave to Abraham in Genesis 15 was fulfilled four hundred years later when the children of Israel were delivered out of Egypt by God using Moses and many miracles.

I think the whole way in which this story happened was ordained by God to show the children of Israel and the rest of the world His glory and trustworthiness. Understand the story of the Jews coming out of Egypt is a story of prediction and deliverance by prophecy and miracles that glorified God. God deserves glory because He alone is God, but He uses His glory for our benefit because we are drawn to Him when we see His glory, such as in the story of the Jews' deliverance from Egypt. We see the glory today through the stories of the Bible, and we are drawn to God. Who else can predict something and then fulfill it centuries later? Seeing God's glory starts faith and trust and salvation. God is trustworthy enough to keep His words that were spoken to Abraham, even though those words were spoken almost 650 years before the Jews came out of Egypt.

Remember My Love

The single most common and frequently reappearing reminder in the Bible is the reminder to the Jews about their deliverance from Egypt. God has reminded them of this story constantly through the rest of the Bible. He reminds them about Joseph and how he came to be in Egypt. He reminds them about Moses, the deliverer and lawgiver. God reminds them about the plagues and the firstborn dying in the land of Egypt. God reminds them how they came out of Egypt after four hundred years of captivity and how the seas parted and the children of Israel passed over on dry ground while Pharaoh's army was drowned in the sea. God even reminds them of their wanderings in the desert for forty years for their unbelief and then going over the Jordan River into the Promised Land.

God kept reminding the children of Israel about that story through the New Testament, seventeen hundred years later. Over 180 times the reminders of Egypt appear throughout the Scriptures after the Israelites came out of Egypt. Every generation throughout the rest of the Bible heard those reminders about the sure testimonies of God. There is a reminder even in Stephen's speech in the book of Acts when Stephen was before the high priest and the council of Jews. In Acts7:6–7, Stephen even acknowledged the prophecy God gave to Abraham in Genesis 15:

> And God spake on this wise, "That his seed should sojourn in a strange land; and that they should bring them into bondage, and entreat them evil four hundred years. And the nation to whom they shall be in bondage to will I judge, said God: and after that shall they come forth, and serve me in this place."

Stephen went on to talk about the selling of Joseph, Joseph being delivered out of all his afflictions, his brothers coming to buy grain, and so on. The story of Israel's enslavement and deliverance is a common thread through the rest of the Scriptures, reminding the Jews of how much they are loved by a God who did so much for them.

Look at all of the feasts Israel celebrates year after year. One of them is celebrated because of what happened while the Jews were in the process of being delivered from Egypt; it is called Passover, because it celebrates when the angel of death passed over the Jews and slew all the firstborn of Egypt. The next feast is called the feast of unleavened bread and it is celebrated right after Passover. The feast of unleavened bread is also celebrated to remind the Jews of the story of their deliverance from Egypt. The Jews had to bake bread in a hurry before leaving Egypt so they had food for their journey, so they left out the leaven (yeast) while making their bread. All of the feasts serve as reminders of the special covenant relationship the Jews have with God.

Reminders Prove Love

Why does God keep reminding His people of what He did? Parents know the reason very well. Parents often speak reminders to show their love for their child and to prove their love so that the relationship between parent and child will prosper. Reminders are not designed to hurt or nag the child; they are spoken to remind the child how much he or she is loved. Do you remember when I did this for you? Do you remember when I did that for you? Remember when we did this together? You see how much I have done for you to prove that I love you? I have done so much to prove my love for you, so you shouldn't think that I don't love you. We should always be in a loving relationship.

You show your love for your child by doing things for him or her; the reminders are spoken so that your child will not forget how much you have done for him or her, proving that he or she is loved. The reminders keep coming because they are a part of God's love for everyone. God reminded the Jews in this way many, many times after they came out of Egypt.

It is common for children who grow up without a father in the home, and who rarely, if ever, communicate with him, to think that their father wants nothing to do with them. Without the father's presence in the home constantly reminding their children about his love, the children are neglected. A child neglected in this way may ask, "Why are other things so much more important to my dad than me?" God never lets His children think that way because God keeps reminding His children of what He did for them to prove His love for them. Those reminders keep coming to establish and enhance the relationship. God is inextricably tied to us in covenant relationship through His Word. The reminders serve to prove His love for us so we will remember all He has done. The reminders bond us together with the Lord

> Bless the Lord O my soul and all that is within me, bless his holy name. Bless the Lord O my soul, and forget not all his blessings. (Ps. 103:1–2)

I believe that God ordained the whole story of the Egyptian experience for the Jews so He could prove His love to them. God is glorified in the whole story of Egypt and the Israelites' deliverance. God has all the glory because He is God, but does God have a need to be glorified? I don't think so, but we have a need to see God be glorified. We need to see Him glorified so we will be drawn to trust in Him. I think God knows this, and He created many proofs of who He is and what He has done so that when we see these proofs, we will know that He is God and will be drawn into relationship with Him. I believe this is the reason why prophecy exists at all—to draw us into relationship with our loving Creator. God made the whole story of the Jews in Egypt happen so that centuries later we would see Him glorified in the Jews' deliverance and would come to have faith and trust in Him as our Lord and God in relationship.

And because he loved thy fathers, therefore he chose their seed after them, and brought thee out in his sight with his mighty power out of Egypt. (Deut. 4:37)

CHAPTER 7
Preparations from Prophecy

A s noted before, the subject of prophecy is so diverse that it is hard to see everything at once that prophecy brings to our faith. There are so many examples of prophecy being used and benefited by in so many of the Bible stories throughout the Bible. Prophecy is for our benefit, our use, and our edification. It is for affirmation and purification. There are places in the Bible where a prophecy has caused a response, and in other places, it has demanded a response before consequences for sin brought punishment.

Are there examples in the Bible of people who God warned to be prepared for something coming? Of course there are many, but certainly the best and sometimes most neglected preparations are those in our heart, making it ready before God as though we may pass through the doorway of death at any moment and find ourselves standing before His throne of judgment. This is the most important preparation we can make, and its importance can't be stressed enough.

In the following Scripture references, we have some very well-known Bible stories. Many of them are stories of preparation in response to knowing the future either by a prophecy or by an interpretation of a prophetically based dream. The people in these stories received these warnings *only* because their hearts were right before God. It was only because these people were righteous before these events happened that they had the chance to prepare for a coming event. No obedient faith meant that people had no idea of what is coming. Not watching meant that no preparations were made. No idea of about prophecy meant suffering or death.

Noah prepared the ark because God saw that man was corrupted throughout the whole world (Gen. 3:12–13). In Genesis 19:1–29, we read the story of Lot, Abraham's nephew who was brought out of the city before the destruction of Sodom and Gomorrah. Another well-known story of preparation in response to prophecy is in Genesis 41:1–36 and the story of Joseph in Egypt. Because of Pharaoh's dream and Joseph's interpretation of that dream, Egypt stored grain to prepare for the time of drought and famine. Egypt and the surrounding nations were saved, including Joseph's family. God created the seven years of plenty and the drought to bring the seven lean years of harvest to cause famine. Why? I think it was to let everyone know that He is faithful. Every kernel of grain the people stored during those seven years of plenty they stored because of a prophetic dream implanted in Pharaoh while he slept. Every kernel of grain the people ate during the seven years of drought and famine was a reminder of Joseph's interpretation of Pharaoh's prophetic dream that came from the Almighty. God was glorified in the eyes of many people and nations, all because of prophecy.

If we believe the story of Jonah is just about the prophet being swallowed by a great fish, then we have totally missed the point of the story. The story of Jonah is the greatest story of prophecy in the entire Bible because the people of Nineveh responded to Jonah's prophetic words, repented, and started relationship with the living God.

The wise men followed a star to the Messiah and (Matt. 2:1–12) were warned in a dream not to return to Herod. They were probably saved from death at the hand of Herod. Many people saw the star in the evening sky that the wise men saw. Many people may've wondered at it, but only the wise men knew it was the star of the Messiah, and they made the long journey to find the King of the Jews and give Him gifts. Mary and Joseph were warned in Joseph's dream to take Jesus into Egypt to escape Herod's death sentence for Jesus.

In the book of Acts (12:27–30), there is a short story of some prophets who came from Jerusalem to Antioch, and one of them prophesied about a coming famine, so they send aid before the famine to the brethren in Judea by the hand of Paul and Barnabas. These are but a few of the many stories where righteous people were warned to make preparations because of a prophecy

You can see that an obedient faith and the purposes of God saved all these people from suffering or death. All of these examples are mostly physical preparations in response to knowing the future by prophecy or interpretation of dreams. Building an ark, storing grain, going out of a city, repenting for sin, taking a long trip to follow a star, moving to Egypt, and sending aid before a famine are all responses to prophecy. All the people in these stories benefited from knowing the prophecy. All these righteous people had understanding about what was going to happen because of prophecy. The people in all these stories knew the Lord and understood His voice when He spoke. Their actions required faith and obedience and sometimes a quick response.

Without faith and obedience, these people would've missed what was coming. The Lord can prosper the righteous in any crisis. On the other hand, if your heart isn't right before the Lord, you won't have a clue about what's coming. Psalms 127:1 says, "Except the Lord build the house, they labour in vain that build it: except the Lord keep the city, the watchmen waketh but in vain." I don't care how many preparations are made; unless you are committed and obedient to the Lord, all your preparations are for nothing.

How do we respond to prophecy in practical ways today? One response to prophecy I have heard of lately by one pastor is very well suited to believers. Some Christians believe the end times will be filled with a lot of natural disasters, earthquakes, and so on that will take place around the world. People who are living in an area where a disaster strikes will need disaster relief workers to come and help them. Relief workers will do triage, search and rescue, give medical aid, distribute supplies, provide temporary shelter, counsel people about their loss, and so on. This pastor wants to see as many Christians as possible trained as disaster relief workers for the purpose of helping hurting people with their suffering and telling them about the love Jesus has for them. I just love that response, and I think that it is good and wise response to the prophetic. It is a response that spreads the gospel, helps people, changes lives, and glorifies the Lord.

Some of you will remember back to Y2K and all the problems we thought were going to come upon the world. Many people stored food in anticipation of a possible food distribution meltdown. They wanted to have food to eat in its aftermath. People stored guns and ammunition to protect their families from the people who didn't prepare. Well, all those preparations were for nothing because the much-vaunted Y2K turned out to be nothing after 12:01 a.m. on January 1, 2001, came and went without a hitch.

The one thing absent from Y2K was righteous people saying it was real and to prepare. There was no prophetic word from God telling His children to prepare for this event. Most of the preparations were made in an attitude of *if* it turns out to be bad, then we will be prepared. Y2K may've been a trial run at what may come later, but one thing that is certain is if something is coming that will affect all the nations, then we will hear of it through the righteous and obedient in Christ because God will not surprise the righteous with a surprise tribulation. "Surely the Lord God will do nothing, but he revealeth his secret unto his servants the prophets." Amos 3:7 is saying that the Lord will do nothing without first revealing it to His servants the prophets.

We respond to prophecy not with fear but with a trusting anticipation. We anticipate the Lord will move to fulfill all the words He has spoken.

If the Lord has already told us about what will happen, doesn't that say He is in control? He knows our future, and He wants us to have the best for our eternal good. Many Christians believe we are living in the end times, and the end-times prophecies can be so scary, but we have trust and not fear when we see these things begin to come to pass.

Christians tend to live separated lives of faith from the rest of the world. Historically we have sequestered ourselves away to live in isolated groups, in monasteries and nunneries. We still do it today. We have Christian retreats and worship behind closed doors on Sundays. The ancient Jews did it too. The Qumran settlement where the Dead Sea Scrolls were found was a religious community that lived near the Dead Sea. They lived apart and away from what they perceived as a corrupted religious system in Jerusalem. They lived there before, during, and shortly after the time of Jesus.

This segregation of faith from people who do not have faith is not right. Somehow we must be seen by nonbelievers when we are worshipping, praying, and reading our Bibles in public. Maybe churches could have their services in a city park or on a downtown mall so everyone can see us practicing our faith, front and center. In these end times, we need to have public faith so we can humbly engage people with our faith. We need to live front and center so that our faith will be active in public. A part of the preparations for these end-times prophecies is the evangelism of the whole world. It is God's heart for us when we are saved to bring as many as the Lord will save along with us into the kingdom.

The purpose of the preparations serves the purpose of prophecy, which is to bring people close to God. A barn raising is a good example of how preparations can bring people together. All your neighbors come with single purpose to help. It was the same in Bible times. Imagine for a moment that you are a member of Noah's family. It is a dangerous time and place because violence had filled the earth. You know that God has told Noah about what was coming and has directed him to build the ark. The work has been slow, you have been working hard, and you've endured many insults of people who have ridiculed your family for building such a thing. But through it all, there has been a vision around the building of the ark, and the vision has provided unity among your family. The work continues through to the end when the ark is finished. God brings the animals to Noah, and Noah and his family and all the animals go into the ark.

Prophecy directs preparations for coming events. It was true in Noah's time, in Joseph's time as they stored grain in Egypt ,and it was true in the New Testament in the book of Acts.

> And there stood up one of them named Agabus, and signified by the spirit that there should be great dearth [famine] throughout all the world: which came to pass in the days of Claudius Caesar. Then the disciples, every man according to his ability, determined to send relief unto the brethren which dwelt at Judea: Which also they did, and sent it to the elders by the hands of Barnabas and Saul. (Acts11:28–30)

The prophecy came by the Spirit that said there would be famine, and the believers in Antioch sent aid before the famine to the church in Jerusalem. This aid that was sent to Jerusalem was a preparation in response to a prophecy.

It is good to have a few preparations for disasters; even our own government's agency of Homeland Security recommends some preparations in case of natural disasters. Having certain items on hand to endure a power outage or a storm is a wise thing. I know there are certain folks in the church today who see very bad things coming on our economic and national horizon. They have retreats in the wilderness and prepare for an EMP strike on America, a nuclear attack, or a global financial meltdown, and they have made physical and financial preparations for themselves for such events. They stock guns and ammo and gold, and they "harden" their survival retreat against attack. They live up in the woods, far away from anyone. Maybe some of them think they will survive the great tribulation by making all these preparations.

I think this isolation from people or from the world is not what God has called us out to do. Jesus called us to be a light to the world. If we set our light far away from anyone, how will anyone see it? All these survivalist preparations are fear based and not at all what the Lord has called us to be motivated by. We stay in the world but not of the world. We have a front-and-center faith that people will ask us about, and we can respond by telling them about our God. Jesus commanded us to pray that the Lord of the harvest will send forth laborers into His harvest. By building isolated survival retreats, it seems as though some laborers have taken themselves out of the harvest. Remember that God's purpose for prophecy is to build relationship with everyone. Prophecy goes on to fill us with hope from promises made by prophecy to give us a "full tank" of endurance for our faith. And it is by prophecy that we can witness of our faith proving that the Lord exists by His words about the future. If all this is true and the overall purpose for prophecy is to build relationships, then how are isolated survival retreats serving the purpose of God to build those relationships?

The best preparation in anticipation of the end times is in the heart, that we might labor in the kingdom until He finishes our work and calls us home, trusting in the Lord that whatever may come, we are safe in Him. Trust is better than fear, but too often fear voids faith. God already told us what the future holds. Are we going to be afraid when we see it coming? That is like the children of Israel coming out of Egypt by prophecy and many miracles. Once in they were in the wilderness, Moses sent out spies (Num. 13:1–33) to scout out the Promised Land. The report most of the spies brought back negated the vision of the Promised Land for the children of Israel. They didn't trust that the Lord would help them win over their enemies, no matter how tall those giants were in the Promised Land.

Like us today, those ancient people didn't trust the Lord, even after they saw the miracles God did to bring them out of the land of Egypt. They knew about the Promised Land by prophecy; we know about the end times by prophecy. They knew they were promised the land and help from God to possess it. We know that God has told us about the end times and promised us help to go through anything. He will be close, like Psalm 23 says, "The Lord is my shepherd ... Yea though I walk through the valley of the shadow of death, I will fear no evil: for thou art with me." Will we be like the former slaves from Egypt and become fearful of what is coming? No, because we know that God will be with us.

Chapter 8

Satan's Purpose for Prophecy

We often forget that when God has a purpose for something, our enemy has an opposite agenda. If God's purpose for prophecy is to build relationships, then Satan's purpose for prophecy is to destroy relationships. When Satan attacks the things of God, he attacks the things that do the most damage and hurt God's people. Satan attacks something that is precious and essential in the life of the believer whenever he assaults prophecy. He does this to destroy faith in God. Satan attacks prophecy because he wants to prevent Christians from enjoying all the benefits that come from prophecy.

In any battle, an army wants to inflict as much damage on its enemy as possible. The generals will choose the most important target and will strike with surprise, speed, and ferocity to inflict the maximum hurt to the enemy. Satan is no different. But Satan attacks not with artillery, bombers, and soldiers; he attacks prophecy with counterfeits, ridicule, fear, and shame. These are Satan's weapons of choice in his war on the church. From so much evidence of Satan's attacks in our media, we should know that Satan is trying to destroy something that has so much value for our faith. Satan attacks something that has so much benefit in it for our faith.

Satan abhors seeing Christians knowing and enjoying the benefits of prophecy. Satan attacks first by ridicule, showing some weird media-generated image of someone who tries to tell the future who is easy to ridicule. Then he directs his hate-filled attack toward the church when there are date prediction failures, such as when someone predicts a date for the return of Jesus or the rapture (another reason to not predict dates). Satan tries to put the church on a hotbed of shame. The church has responded by avoiding one of the very things that is vital to our faith. Finally Satan offers counterfeits to confuse as many as possible so finding the truth is difficult.

Negative Images Close Doors

Whenever the media portrays someone who is telling the future, what kind of an image do they show? That's easy because it is a well-known stereotype. It's usually a bearded, wild-eyed, unstable person carrying a sandwich board, saying meaningless things, and scaring people. This image is shown on TV, in movies, and in magazines. It may be a person dressed as a media-stereotyped gypsy, looking into a crystal ball, and reading the lines on someone's palm, or they wear a sandwich board saying, "Repent, the end is near."

These media-generated, self-glorifying, fanatical people scare others by their actions and say strange things that make no sense. Who would ever want to be associated with those images? Anyone connected with that would also be looked at as being unstable merely by association. I think that at least in part, the church's response has been avoidance to prevent ridicule and shame. The church wants nothing to do with that image. It is too easy to ridicule and be relegated to the supermarket tabloid newspapers, alongside stories about vampires, UFOs, and conspiracy theories. We have seen many times in the media where some fringe group has predicted the end of the world, the rapture, or some other biblical event, and the date came and went without any fulfillment of their prediction. But in our avoidance of the fake and deceptive, we have also sidestepped the real, the true, and the valuable.

Bible schools by and large do not have courses on prophecy, and the few that do have it usually offer it only as an elective. Pastoral students graduate from Bible school untaught in prophecy, so there are few pastors who feel comfortable teaching about prophecy, let alone knowing of its purpose and benefits.

I believe Satan is very satisfied with himself. He has gotten many Christians to close the door on the study of prophecy. The ranks of people who speak on Bible prophecy today are filled with self-endorsed counterfeits, glory seekers, and terrible teaching, and they eagerly promote themselves as prophets or apostles. They promote themselves only for power and control. Satan has confused the truth with many deceivers, counterfeits, false doctrines, and debates. What pastor would want to bring all that trouble into the church by teaching about it? We have created the debates by not teaching it. The congregation fends for themselves by studying any book or listening to sermons other than by their own pastor. That is how we get so many different opinions about prophecy in the church. If the church taught it to their own congregations, then that would unify opinions and reduce the controversy.

I must admit, as I mentioned before, that when I bring up prophecy with someone or in a group, I often get those blank stares and a, "That's nice" response. It's not that what is being said is a bad interpretation or a misapplication; it's just that people do not know about prophecy and are befuddled upon hearing about it. It is a closed-door response to prophecy. Although Christians who read their Bibles quite a bit have a better grasp of prophecy, even they have little understanding about God's purpose for it and have a tendency to be wary of it.

Attacks on the Watchmen

The church believes that the Lord could return soon, but the church also has a tendency to not watch for fulfillment. It is like the watchmen on those ancient walls around Jerusalem looking for anything afar off that would affect the city. They were on duty twenty-four/seven, diligently scanning the countryside around the city. Christians today are like those watchmen on the ancient walls of Jerusalem. But we've lost something today. We do believe that the Lord will return, but we don't watch. It would be like the watchmen on the walls around Jerusalem believing that an enemy could come at any time but coming down off the walls and going their way. If you were to ask them if they still believed an enemy could come, they would reply yes, but they've stopped watching long ago.

It is not socially acceptable to talk about the future in public. The watchmen have been shamed away from watching. This is an attack of the enemy; it is a gate of hell that must be confronted and broken down in the church today. The area of prophecy is for God's people alone, and the enemy has claimed so much of it for himself. It is time for the church to take this territory out of the pit of hell and use it for the kingdom of God.

Avoidance Promotes Neglect

Prophecy avoiders today do not know or understand its many benefits. It is like working at a dream job with every benefit imaginable and all paid for by the company. The employees have ample opportunity to take advantage of all the rich benefits but almost never use any of them. They miss out on what makes the job so great. We as Christians do the same thing when we ignore prophecy. Because Satan has been successful in the media to taint some of the benefits of our faith, we don't go and just enjoy the benefits. It is because we see the source of those benefits so easily ridiculed and tainted. Why should the words of God be avoided, disdained, and ignored by so many in the church today? It is at least in part because of this ridicule and shaming by Satan. If prophecy is being attacked by Satan, so often that alone says it has a high value for our faith. If our enemy hates it so much, then it must have an important place in the life of every believer.

On one side we have the world's view of prophecy—what the world makes of all this—and then we have the prevailing Christian view as it is written and preached about today. On one side there is God, who gives the words of the future, and on the other side are people who are proponents of everything weird about those prophecies.

Remember, prophecy is the Word of God. It is not our word, and we did not create it. God does not need to speak prophecy for His benefit; He lives continually with the knowledge of all things. God speaks prophecy for our benefit. God gives us His Word for our benefit. When we look at the words God has spoken, we are studying the words that have come from God. Is it so important to avoid a portion of prophecy because it has a controversial past that we actually disdain the words of God because of the ridicule of the world?

Think of it—Christians who practice avoidance of so much prophetic Scripture is the very thing that delights Satan. Anything that comes from God should be looked at as pure and meant for our eternal good. The first-century church heard and experienced prophecy quite a bit. First John 4:1 says, "Beloved believe not every spirit, but try the spirits, whether they are of God; because many false prophets are gone out into the world." There were "many false prophets" who had gone out into the world to deceive and espouse their false doctrines. The first-century church lived with prophecy from both God and false prophets, and yet they knew what was true. Why has prophecy come to be viewed as a subject that only the unbalanced are into? You don't have to be a weirdo to want to learn about prophecy.

The Ultimate and Least-Known Conspiracy Theory

Are you interested in conspiracy theories, such as how JFK was killed, area 51, chemical trails, black helicopters, and government secrets? Do you know that the biggest and most important conspiracy theory of all time is completely ignored by even the most astute conspiracy theorists? They are completely clueless about the biggest conspiracy theory in all of history, and even they are fooled by its lies and its very successful cover up.

The biggest conspiracy of all is a deception put out by Satan for thousands of years that puts everyone in the world subject to eternal damnation. It is Satan's intent to deceive the world and destroy faith in God. It is Satan's intent to one day rule the earth and be worshipped by everyone. Satan manufactures so many lies for the whole earth to believe. Here are only a few of them: There are many ways to God, including believing in yourself as God; God is dead; it's only a fetus; I'm a good person, so I'll go to heaven; I have been to college, so I'm smarter than everyone else; religion is just a silly superstition; I have to be really good so God will love me; I have to clean up my act first before I come to God; God can't forgive me for what I have done; man can make the world a peaceful place; we evolved from monkeys; the Bible is filled with contradictions and fairy tales; morality is all relative; there is no such thing as sin; God doesn't love me; science will solve humankind's problems; Jesus has already returned; and on and on the lies go. The whole earth is filled with people who believe this stuff. Christians believe some of these things too.

Being deceived has nothing to do with intellect or education because it is a spiritual deception. No one will admit he or she is deceived because when you are deceived, you just don't know it until the truth from God's Word comes along and sheds light on Satan's lies. Neither force of intellect nor depth of education can defeat this spiritual deception from Satan. In John 8:44, Jesus told us about Satan's lies.

> Ye are of your father, the Devil, and the lusts of your father ye will do. He was a murder from the beginning, and abode not in the truth, because there was no truth in him. When

he speaketh a lie, he speaketh of his own: for he is a liar and
the father of it.

Jesus was speaking here to the educated people of Israel. You can only
defeat the burning power of Satan's lies with the fountain of living water
from God's Word. People are deceived because they lack the one thing
that defeats lies and deception: a good and ongoing understanding and
study of the Bible. Now this is a conspiracy theory worth studying,
but you'll only find the true story behind the long history of Satan's
conspiracy to deceive the whole world in the Bible. The only way to
defeat the power of these lies and know the truth is to abide in the
Word of God continually.

Satan has a malicious purpose for biblical prophecy; he uses it to destroy
faith. He uses as many false prophets as possible to make prophecy a
subject so weird that everyone, including, Christians will close the door
on it. Satan has included some prophecy in other religions and cults
too—not for the purpose of proving that religion's authenticity but for
the purpose of confusing God's truth. Satan tries to make the truth
as difficult as possible to know and make the false stand out as more
appealing than the truth.

It's kind of like there is one special tree in the forest. It has a sign on
it that says, "This is God's tree." When the sign was put on that tree,
everyone knew it was God's tree. People drew near to be close to that
tree because they knew it was God's. Satan comes along one day and
is jealous that everyone is worshipping God and gathered around God's
tree. He gets angry and comes to hate all the people who are coming
to God's tree in the forest. Satan puts up signs on many other trees
in that forest to say, "This is God's tree." Now when the people come
to the forest, some of them go to one of the counterfeit trees and think
they are by the true tree of God when they are really by one of Satan's
deceptions. The people start to argue with each other about who is by

the real tree of God. Satan is so filled with delight by confusing so many who are seeking after God.

Deceivers and Date Setting

When you hear people say there are many ways to God, you must understand that a lie has just been spoken. It is a lie because it contradicts John 14:6, Acts 4:12, and 1 Timothy 2:5. John 14:6 says, "Jesus saith unto him, I am the way, the truth, and the life: no man cometh to the Father, but by me." Acts 4:12 says, "Neither is there salvation in any other: for there is none other name under heaven given among men, whereby we must be saved." First Timothy 2:5 says, "For there is one God and one mediator between God and men, the man Christ Jesus."

If Satan can't destroy the truth, he will confuse the truth. No other religious work has such an overwhelming prophetic proving factor like the Bible. Satan appeals to the flesh and offers glory and attention to the religious. They wear robes or have some outward sign that identifies them as belonging to a special group. They glorify themselves with self-stitched-on labels like "prophet" or "apostle." They lift themselves up as being closer to God than anyone else and may even say that they say that they hear God's own voice. It is as Jesus said about the Pharisees in Matthew 6:5, "They have their reward." They do outward things to have the praises of men.

Once when I was younger, I was riding in the back of a pickup and the driver pulled over and picked up a hitchhiker. The young man got into the bed of the pickup with me, and we promptly started talking. He was in a cult called the "holy order of man" and showed me a one-page folded pamphlet he had about the group he was in. This pamphlet had a list of requirements people had to meet in order to join this group. I noticed that one of the requirements was poverty; it said you had to be poor because money was the root of all evil. I told this fellow that the

Bible didn't say money was the root of all evil. He disputed with me, so I showed him the Scripture out of 1 Timothy 6:10 where it says that the *love* of money is the root of all evil. Do you know what this young man did? He took his own pamphlet and a pen, and he crossed out that requirement. Talk about not being committed to your own doctrine. I wish he would have thrown that whole pamphlet away.

There was a man who had a call-in talk show on the radio who set a date of May 21, 2011, for the rapture. Maybe you heard him before that date on the radio. He sounded so serious with his deep, gravelly voice and his date setting. He has set other dates that have been wrong, and he was wrong about this one too. His date predictions go against Scriptures in Matthew 24:36, which says, "But of that day and hour knoweth no man, no, not the angels of heaven, but my Father only." In Luke 12:40, it says, "Be ye therefore ready also; for the Son of man cometh at an hour when ye think not." I wonder how he justified his mistake in his own walk with the Lord now that the dates he has picked have come and gone. Of course he went off claiming another date, and he was wrong about that one too. Either way, people of faith will look foolish, and the church will be blamed. Other religions will be viewed by the unlearned as more appealing to follow than those hypocritical Christians.

The Watchtower Society of Jehovah's witnesses based in Brooklyn, New York, set several dates for the Lord's return [5]. They made announcements for each date. Everyone expected the Lord to return as these dates came, but the dates came and went without the Lord coming. The leadership of the Jehovah's witnesses was very embarrassed by these date-prediction failures and finally set another date in 1914. When the Lord didn't return on that date, they were embarrassed again, so to save themselves all that shame once again, they came out and said He really did return, but only spiritually. They say He is ruling the earth right now. The average Jehovah's Witness has to have faith that the Lord is ruling the earth now, something that can't be proven, and that protects those leaders of Jehovah's Witnesses in Brooklyn. If they believe that is true, then I'm thinking it is not Jesus who is presently ruling this earth; it is someone else.

Of course, their belief is not scriptural. We know that Jesus returns only once. He doesn't return twice or secretly or spiritually. In Matthew 24:24–27 Jesus said,

> For there shall arise false Christs, and false prophets, and shall shew great signs and wonders; insomuch that, if it were possible, they shall deceive the very elect. Behold I have told you before. Wherefore if they shall say unto you, behold he is in the desert; go not forth: behold he is in the secret chambers; believe it not. For as the lightning [light from the sun] goes out of the east and shineth even unto the west; so shall the coming of the Son of man be.

> Behold he cometh with the clouds; and every eye shall see him, and they also which pierced him: and all kindreds of the earth shall wail because of him. Even so, Amen. Revelation 1:7

Jesus will return so that every eye will see Him return, and that includes your eyes and mine. I haven't seen Him return, and I don't think you have either. And on and on it goes.

We do the same thing. Some of you may remember back before 1988 many Christians (this writer included) thought the Lord would likely return or the rapture would happen in that year. We thought that 1988 was the year that He would return because it was forty years—a generation—after Israel became a nation. That heightened expectation was based on a verse repeated in Matthew 24:32–34, Mark 13:28–30, and Luke 21:29–32 where Jesus was talking about a fig tree that puts forth its branches. We knew the fig tree is a national symbol of Israel, and Jesus said that the generation that sees this happen will not pass till all things be fulfilled.

Many of us thought the Lord would return within a generation of 1948 when Israel "put forth its branches" and became a nation again. We thought a generation was forty years, the math was easy, and we would be raptured in 1988. Then the date changed again when Israel took over the ancient part of the city of Jerusalem in 1967. Again applying the forty years in a generation brought us to 2007. Well, it looks like a biblical generation can be up to 120 years (Gen. 6:3). So let's see, 1948 or 1967 plus 120 brings the date to ... huh, never mind!

You will not hear me set any dates for the rapture or return of Jesus. I refuse to set dates for two reasons, both of them scriptural. The first is in Mark 13:32: "But of that day and hour no one knows, not even the angels in heaven, nor the Son but only the Father." Obviously, if the information is known only to the Father and not even by Jesus, then if I set a date, I am claiming superior knowledge to Jesus, and that, folks, I am not willing to do. My second reason is the same verse as mentioned before in Matthew 24:44 where Jesus says, "Therefore be ye also ready: for in such an hour as ye think not the Son of man cometh." It happens at an hour that we think not. The season is ours to know but not the date. Date setting is so unscriptural. Satan loves to set dates for the rapture and the second coming so he can frustrate people of faith. So just say no to date setting or listening to people who do this foolishness.

Stop with That Prophecy

I really don't blame those who stop me from talking about prophecy in mid-sentence, put their hands up in a stop motion, and say, "Sorry, I'm just not into that stuff." I really do understand, but that is not the way that it should be; it's just the way it has become. People should be eager to learn about a subject that takes up over a quarter of all Bible verses, just as they would be eager to learn anything else about the Bible. I confess to you that sometimes when people say that to me,

I think they have been successfully trained to close their understanding to so much of their Bible.

I do pray for my brothers and sisters in Christ to see what they are missing out on. I think of John 14:25–26 where it says:

> These things have I spoken unto you, being yet present with you. But the Comforter, which is the Holy Ghost, whom the Father will send in my name, he shall teach you all things, and bring all things to your remembrance, whatsoever I have said unto you.

The Christians who refuse to look at prophecy might as well say to the Holy Ghost, "Sorry, Holy Spirit, don't bring those prophecies that Jesus spoke to my remembrance. I'm just not into all that prophecy stuff that Jesus and the prophets spoke about." I believe the person who is not into prophecy truly misses out on its many benefits, but unfortunately, they have turned off their minds to the Holy Spirit and receiving something prophecy related to their remembrance. I do believe we have an enemy that rejoices when we close our understanding to so much of the Bible's truths.

There is a story in Luke 4:15–30 where Jesus went to home to Nazareth and went into His synagogue. That day Jesus was on His synagogue's schedule to read a certain portion of Scripture. It turned out to be a prophecy about the Messiah. The Scripture Jesus read is from Isaiah 61:1:

> The Spirit of the Lord is upon me, because he hath anointed me to preach the gospel to the poor; he hath sent me to heal the broken hearted, to preach deliverance to the captives and recovering of sight to the blind, to set at liberty them that are bruised, to preach the acceptable year of the Lord.

Jesus handed the book to the minister and sat down. Sitting down was the way teachers taught, so He sat to teach. Jesus said, "This day is this Scripture fulfilled in your ears." Jesus was telling them that the Scripture He just had read was about Him. Jesus was telling them He was the long-awaited Messiah. He told them some other things, and the people in that synagogue were outraged. They forced Jesus out of the city to a hill to throw Him down head first to kill Him.

Here was the long-awaited Messiah sitting right there in front of them, and although they were all looking for the Messiah, when He came, they couldn't believe it. The Jews in that synagogue were filled with wrath, and they wanted to kill Jesus. Imagine looking and longing for something for so long that when you finally find it, you can't believe it, and you become so angry you want to destroy it. I'm sure these Jews were looking for the Messiah and most likely knew all the Scriptures about the Messiah. But when it came time to actually believe that one of their own was the Messiah, they couldn't believe it. They had a belief in the coming of the Messiah, but they were not looking for fulfillment. They had faith, but they were not watching with an eye to see fulfillment. Jesus wasn't saying anything weird or preaching a bad doctrine; they just had unbelief.

Sometimes we Christians are like the Jews in that synagogue with Jesus. At the very least, we are skeptical about a prophecy that may have come to pass. Christians who have been with the Lord for a long while and even believe that we are living in the end times are sometimes the hardest people to convince that a particular sign or prophecy has come true. Please understand this: believing we are living in the end times is very different than watching for prophetic fulfillment. Believing without expectant watchfulness is like an astronomer who never looks up at the evening sky and never uses a telescope. Expectancy without the anticipation that watchfulness produces can become lukewarm in its hope.

It is completely astonishing to us that any prophecies would possibly be fulfilled in our lifetime. Ask any believer if he or she believes that Jesus is coming, and he or she would say yes. Most believers would say that they believe we are in the end times. But tell believers of a prophetic fulfillment, and they would wag their heads in unbelief. They have at some point in their faith stopped watching for signs and fulfillments, much to Satan's delight. The church must be held accountable for this lack of watching, but more than being held accountable, we must change.

I'm not saying here that we should run to every wind of doctrine and embrace it or believe everything we hear or all that we read on the Internet. Of course not; Satan would love to give the church more false doctrine by carelessly throwing our faith haphazardly into any doctrine we hear about. We test new things we hear and examine them closely to see if they match up against the scrutiny of the rest of Scripture, like it says to do in 1 John 4:1.

A part of every church should be some sort of council to hear new doctrines and examine them to prove them. This is a good way to protect the flock from those things that are false. I think the first-century church had something like this because of the following Scripture from 1 John 4:1: "Beloved, believe not every spirit, but try the spirits whether they are of God: because many false prophets are gone out in the world." We should search the Scriptures to see if something new we hear matches up with the rest of the Bible. The Bereans did this in Acts 17:11: "These were more noble than those in Thessalonica, in that they received the word with all readiness of mind, and searched the Scriptures daily, whether those things were so." They searched the Scriptures in the Berean church to prove what they should believe in. Every church should have a well-experienced new doctrine testing department for their congregations.

We do fail to watch for the small stuff, like the star that the wise men followed. The star was not the fulfillment of any prophecy; the fulfillment was the birth of the Messiah-Jesus. That star the wise men followed was something the Lord showed just those wise men to follow to find the

Messiah. Imagine Simeon the righteous man in Luke 2:25-35 denying what the Holy Spirit was showing him the day he saw Jesus in the temple? No, this couldn't be the Messiah! That would be a lack of faith in the ability of God to fulfill His own words.

If you hear something new about a Bible doctrine and are not so sure about it, immediately put the brakes on. Slow down, and don't take it in as fact and put your faith in it. Satan loves those quick decisions to accept falsehoods as truth. Talk with other Christians who read their Bible a lot, and bounce that new doctrine off them. Tell them of things you have read on the Internet, heard on the street corner, or from the media. Sometimes it won't sound like false doctrine, but it will be a doctrine out of the pit of hell. Those who are avid readers of the Bible will be a great help to avoid doctrinal falsehoods. Read your Bible because it is truth, and it will teach you everything that is good and acceptable. Remember also that God will keep you safe. Have a heart that is always willing to be led by the Holy Spirit to guide you into all truth. "Howbeit when he, the Spirit of truth, is come he will guide you into all truth: for he shall not speak of himself; but whatsoever he shall hear, that shall he speak: and he will shew you things to come" (John 16:13).

God is working right now in very detailed and unseen ways to bring an end to this world and to bring with Him an everlasting righteousness and start our eternity with Him. Don't miss out because you are not actively watching for it. Don't let your hope grow dim because you don't study the very thing that keeps your hope strong, which is prophecy. Don't have a weakened faith because you are tired of waiting and your patience is wearing thin waiting for the Lord.

Can you be saved if you know nothing about the end times or prophecy? Of course you can! Can you have a faith in the Lord that saves you without knowing about prophecy? Yes! But prophecy brings so many benefits to the life of faith. Why starve yourself while you are waiting for the Lord? Don't try to cross the desert without water. The study of prophecy acquaints us with the benefits list and gives us hope. Do we need a strong hope in these times to keep us going in our faith? Absolutely yes!

Hope is like water in the canteen while trying to cross that desert. When we know about fulfilled prophecy, we see the faithfulness of God. When we study the many prophecies that show us an abundant inheritance for our faith, we strengthen our hope. So yes, you can be saved without knowing about prophecy. It may seem to the unwise that the desert can be crossed without taking a lot of water, but the sand in the middle of that desert will swallow them up after their death from thirst. Not studying the source of our hope in Christ makes our hope an abstract thing and makes it weak. Who would want to make their faith weak? Christians do it all the time when we don't study the source of our hope to make it strong.

I'm sure God will continue to fulfill prophecy whether we're watching or not. Simply believing that we are in the end times is not enough. Jesus spoke of watching for signs of His coming seventeen times. It is an act of obedience to keep an active watch for the signs and fulfillments. Again using the ancient watchmen as an example, they were upon the walls in all the cities and towns in Israel, and they actually had to watch for danger coming. Christians who do not watch are like watchmen who come down off the wall and go their way. The watchmen leave those walls and go live their lives and still believe that an enemy can come, but they have grown tired of all that watching and waiting. They believe it is just not that important anymore to watch. God help us!

Be open to watching and to prophetic fulfillment but not to the point of accepting something false. Remember, whatever the signs you may think are being fulfilled, they must follow the rest of the Word and good teaching. It is easy to pull one thread of Scripture out of the tapestry of the Bible and build a huge doctrine—a much different looking tapestry—on that one thread. Many people have done this and built false teachings on it, but when you put that thread back up against the original tapestry it came from, you lose all your false doctrine because none of the false doctrine fits in with the rest of Scripture. Do not be doctrinal lone wolves; share your ideas with others who are avid readers of the word. Share your thoughts of a possible prophetic fulfillment with others who are watching for prophetic fulfillment before committing yourself to believing in it. Don't commit to it before it is examined and proven true.

Putting our faith in something is like the transmission in a car. Have the things that you know well and solidly believe in moving forward like having your transmission in drive. Put your transmission in neutral when you are not so sure about something new you have just heard about. Put your transmission into reverse when you hear about something that you know is false; back up and get away from it. Too many cults start with these lone wolves having a prophecy, a "revelation," or a misinterpretation of Scripture that just does not fit in with the rest of the Bible. They lead unlearned people into destruction

Some of you may recall a man named David Berg. He lived in southern California and went to a Bible study at a Salvation Army building. He started to condemn the people in the Bible study for having long hair; eventually he left the Bible study, renamed himself Moses David, and started a cult called the Children of God. Among other things, his disciples used to sit around in a big circle chanting, "I hate my mother, I hate my father." They took one of those scriptural threads out of Luke 14:26 from the tapestry of the Bible. In that verse Jesus said, "If a man come to me and hate not his father and his mother, and wife, and children and brethren, and sisters, yea and his own life also he cannot be my disciple." Of course the word hate in this verse is a poor translation in the King James, which means to love less. We know Jesus was saying here that He must be first in our lives, before any other person. In the Children of God cult, they built some of their dogma on this one thread, but put that thread back against the tapestry of the whole Bible and back against the fifth commandment in Exodus 20:12 that says to honor your mother and father then their teachings become very, very obviously wrong.

Unfortunately today we have no person who is acknowledged nationally as a prophet. We would call Billy Graham an evangelist or Rick Warren a pastor, but no one is acknowledged nationwide as a prophet. We have no one who is a prophet advising a king, president, or prime minister. No government official is a prophet, like Daniel or Joseph, who could interpret prophetic dreams. Sadly, there is no positive image in our national media of anyone in government who is an avid Bible reader or who prays daily. The media portrays Bible-believing Christians as irrelevant, superstitious, ignorant, or imbalanced. Certainly those of us who are into prophecy fall into the imbalanced category.

We have no national example of a prophecy spoken by a prophet and coming true like Israel did many times in its history. Satan has tainted the whole subject of Bible prophecy and largely muted its proponents in the mainstream media. I say it is time here in this place for this spiritual gate to fall and for this territory to be taken back by the church; it is ours to claim. We can take legitimate prophecy back from the hand of the enemy. It is ours to use, experience, and be blessed by with its study and understanding. Satan cannot stand against a committed church that is seeking the truths of God in the Bible.

Let's see what it takes for a person to be a prophet of God in the Bible and not a deceiver and false prophet. For the sake of simplicity, I'll combine both Old and New Testaments to describe this. I'm offering a list of criteria for Bible prophets to be considered prophets.

1. A prophet could be a man or a woman, and his or her character must be above reproach (Gen. 30:24, 1 Sam. 2:1–10, Luke 1:41–45, Acts 2:17, 1 Samuel 3:19–20, Daniel 1:8, 1 John 2:29).

2. Prophets must have a record of faith in God and in the Lord Jesus Christ (1 Sam. 3:19–20, Dan. 1:8)

3. They must be born again in Christ (1 Peter 1:23).

4. They must be filled with the Holy Spirit (2 Kings 2:9, Judges 6:34, 1 Sam. 16:13).

5. They had to have a record of obedience to the Lord and to His Word (1 John 5:2–5).

6. They can't show signs and wonders for the purpose of leading others to serve other gods (Deut. 13:1–10).

7. True prophets served and glorified only the Lord God and received no compensation for their work (Num. 22:1–18).

8. Their prophecies ultimately were intended to lead the people back into covenant relationship with God (Jonah 3:1–10).

9. The prophecies they spoke came true (Isa. 7:14, Matt. 1:18–25).

10. In the New Testament, prophets had to acknowledge that Jesus had come in the flesh (1 John 2:21–23, 4:2).

11. True prophets had to love everyone as Jesus did (1 John 4:20–21).

12. Everything they say must align with all Scripture and not be one shade off (2 Tim. 3:16, 2 John 1:9).

13. They must not be lone wolves, not being a part of a church (1 Sam. 10:10, 1 Kings 18:4, 1 John 2:18–19).

14. They must be humble and not glory seekers (Isa. 57:15).

15. They understood that the messages they brought were more

important than their own lives (Dan. 2:26–28, Jer. 37:11–21, Matt. 5:12).

If all of these things from both the Old and New Testaments about the qualifications for being a prophet are met, then their word was still to be judged with scrutiny. Not every prophet who spoke in the name of the Lord was stoned to death if what they said didn't come to pass. Deuteronomy 18:22 left them a way out. It says, "When a prophet speaketh in the name of the Lord, if the thing follow not, not come to pass, that is the thing which the Lord hath not spoken, but the prophet hath spoken it presumptuously: thou shall not be afraid of him." So if everything else in a prophet's life said he was a follower of the Lord, then he was not stoned if what he prophesied did not come true. On the other hand, if a prophet spoke a prophecy that led to serving false gods or went after some false doctrine, then that prophet was to be stoned to death. There is a difference between a true prophet who speaks presumptuously and a false prophet speaking for God who led people away from God.

Why was the penalty for a false prophet so harsh? I believe it was because God's words about the future were so special that when a false prophet spoke for God, it was met with death. Only God can tell the future with complete accuracy. For a false prophet to say that he is speaking for God and then have his predictions fail in their fulfillment makes people turn away from God and prevents relationship with the Almighty. If the purpose for prophecy is for relationship, then false prophecy prevents relationship. False prophecy makes people ridicule the prophet who spoke it, and they are not drawn to the Lord; they are pushed further away from God.

In the minds of people, false prophecy proves nothing, maybe even reinforcing their idea that there is no God. Everything God does promotes relationship with Him, but false prophets and their deceptions destroy that which is the heart of God. The penalty for pushing people away from God is death. Sin separates us from God, but sin is also a deceiver that never leads us to the truth. Sin greatly boasts itself to be truth, but it has nothing to do with the ways of God. In ancient times, as listed above, there were scriptural laws to being a prophet, with severe consequences for being a false prophet or speaking something that wasn't from God.

A simple reading from God's Word reveals that a true prophet of God can make mistakes, but a false prophet has intentions of leading people away from God. Deuteronomy 13:1–5 says:

> If there arise among you a prophet, or a dreamer of dreams, and giveth thee a sign of a wonder, And the sign or the wonder come to pass, whereof he spake unto thee, saying, Let us go after other gods, which thou, hast not known, and let us serve them: Thou shalt not harken unto the words of that prophet, or that dreamer of dreams: for the Lord your God proveth you to know whether ye love the Lord your God with all your heart and with all your soul.

Often the gods people in the Bible served were served according to their flesh and not contrary to their flesh. In other words, God wants us to serve Him contrary to what we want to do. The false gods in the Bible fed people's evil desires. It was easy to serve other gods because serving false gods felt good because it was sin. On one hand, the living God commands that we serve Him contrary to our sinful nature with the promise of extreme rewards later. False gods and their prophets give people instant gratification of their sinful nature, with the sure consequence of separation from the true God for eternity.

Is a prophet's life perfect? No! Certainly Jonah had issues with unforgiveness because he wanted the people of Nineveh to suffer God's wrath. Isaiah was in the throne room of God and confesses he is a man of unclean lips and he comes from a people of unclean lips (Isa. 6:5). David was most certainly a prophet, and he committed adultery and had Uriah killed so he could cover up his sin and have Uriah's wife Bathsheba (2 Sam. 11:1–24).

We are told to test the spirits. "Beloved believe not every spirit, but try the spirits whether they are of God: because many false prophets are gone out into the world" (1 John 4:1). Pride and the desire for control and fame have been the watermark of many false prophets. So if someone didn't meet all these criteria for a prophet, then he or she was readily accepted by Satan as a false prophet and put to work against the kingdom of God. God, help us to see through the deception of Satan to see what is true and comes from You and what is false (also look up Deut. 13:1–5, 18:19–22, and Jer. 28).

Satan's purpose for prophecy is to make as many counterfeits as possible so that the truth is not clear. Satan's purpose for prophecy is to destroy, control, and prevent people from coming to know the truth and enjoy its benefits. Satan's purpose for prophecy is to destroy relationship with God.

Chapter 9

Thus Says the Lord

One of the things I have come to learn and admire about the Lord is the sometimes-subtle ways in which He proves Himself to us. He proves He alone is God by history and archeology, by prophecy, by the Word, in nature and in His creation, by the testimony of the Holy Spirit, and in many other ways. He often reveals Himself to us in ways that we slowly learn to see and abundantly proves who He is for our benefit. These things are a part of the testimonies of God. All the testimonies of God are shown to prove who He is for the purpose of creating a relationship with you and me. As we look closer at the way the Lord works, we understand that there is much more to what He does than a casual look will reveal.

One of the many subtle ways He reveals evidence of His nature is in the way prophecy is spoken. Did you ever notice there is a difference in the way all the prophets prophesied and the way in which Jesus prophesied? Both the prophets and Jesus spoke about the future but with a difference. When prophets prophesied, the words they spoke came from God. They were not speaking for themselves. Many times we read about the word of the Lord coming to a prophet. Genesis 15:1, "The word of the Lord came to Abraham." That one is from one of the earliest records of that phrase. Isaiah 1:1 says, "The vision of Isaiah the son of Amoz, which he saw concerning Judah and Jerusalem in the days of Uzziah, Jotham, Ahaz and Hezekiah kings of Judah." Isaiah goes on to tell about that vision.

Often the words that came to a prophet would also tell the prophet who to go and tell the prophecy to. Sometimes the word of God was for a king or to a nation or an individual; the prophet was a messenger to deliver the word of God. Prophets made sure that anyone listening to the prophecy understood that they were not speaking their own words; they were speaking for God. The way in which they separated their own words from the words that they were speaking for God was to first say, "This is what the word of God says," or by saying, "Thus says the Lord" or "Hear the word of the Lord." What followed was from the Lord. Ancient diplomats and statesmen did the same thing; they were representatives of their king or government to deliver messages for their government. We see Isaiah, Jeremiah, Ezekiel, and all the prophets using this, "Thus says the Lord" kind of statement before they spoke for God. They gave God the glory for what was about to be spoken. We see it used many times in the Bible.

"I Say to You"

Did you know that Jesus never said, "Thus says the Lord"? The Bible never says the word of the Lord came to Jesus like it says the word of the Lord came to the prophets. Jesus never said, "Hear the word of the Lord," like so many prophets did before Him. He never said those words indicating He was speaking for God when declaring future things, not even once. Matthew 26:34 says, "Jesus said unto him, Verily I say unto thee, that this night, before the cock crow, thou shalt deny me thrice." There is no, "Thus saith the Lord" kind of a statement in this verse to separate out Jesus' words from the words that God wanted Him to say. Jesus told of the future quite often, never once using that phrase to separate the message of God. Why? The Bible never says the word of the Lord came to Jesus because the word of God never came to Jesus in the same way that it came to the prophets. He never said, "Thus says the Lord" because He spoke on His own authority. When Jesus prophesied, He spoke as God, because He is God. He was proving who He was/is to everyone by the way He spoke prophecy. Without

99

God's word spoken to us, we humans can't know the future. God did not make us with that capacity. So when Jesus spoke about the future on His own authority, He was proving He was God.

In Matthew 24:2, Jesus starts to prophesy about the temple's destruction and says, "See ye not all these things? Verily I say unto you, there shall not be left here one stone upon another, that shall not be thrown down." Another example of how Jesus spoke prophecy is in Luke 22:34 where Jesus is speaking to Peter: "And he said, I tell thee, Peter, the cock shall not crow this day before that thou shalt thrice deny that thou knowest me." Jesus spoke prophecy on His own authority as God because He is God.

In Matthew Jesus had just finished the Sermon on the Mount, and Matthew 7:28–29 says, "And it came to pass, when Jesus had ended these sayings, the people were astonished at his doctrine: for he taught them having authority, and not as the scribes." Why did Jesus have authority in His doctrine? It was partly because of the way He spoke to the people. Many of you have read the Sermon on the Mount from Matthew's gospel in chapters 5 through 7. It is a very famous portion of Scripture. The verses in Matthew 5:3–12 are what we know as the Beatitudes. Verses 3–7 say:

> Blessed are the poor in spirit: for theirs is the kingdom of heaven. Blessed are they that mourn: for they shall be comforted. Blessed are the meek for they shall inherit the earth. Blessed are they which do hunger and thirst after righteousness: for they shall be filled. Blessed are the merciful: for they shall obtain mercy.

The Beatitudes go on into verse 13, but these are here as a prime example of prophecy. Believers who have the qualities listed there shall inherit the blessings listed. If you have one or more of those qualities in your faith, then you shall inherit that blessing. Do you know that in the Sermon on the Mount Jesus prophesied no less than twenty-five times, never once saying the phrase, "Thus says the Lord"? The Olivet Discourse in Matthew chapters 24 and 25 is almost all about prophecy. It is true that Jesus spoke the words the Father wanted Him to say (John 7:17), but Jesus had total authority to speak prophecy because He is God! I believe prophecy is in the Bible because God wants us to know what is coming to prepare our hearts by our relationship with Him, but Jesus was proving who He is by the way in which He spoke.

I know that people who learn a different language look for people who speak the same language they are learning. They want to have conversational Spanish or conversational French to practice and become proficient with their new language. Well, the language Jesus spoke was conversational prophecy. His words about the future were blended in with all the other things He said. Now we don't need to study a whole new language to understand what He was saying, but we do need to tune in to how He spoke about the future. That way we will know when He was speaking prophecy even though He didn't use the hallmark, "Thus saith the Lord" when He spoke words that were set in the future.

CHAPTER 10

The Loving Parent

I t is good and proper for loving and wise parents to make all the plans and decisions for their small children. Small children have no basis, no experience for making decisions; they are too young. They don't know the difference between a good decision and a bad one. You could truthfully say that little children were born yesterday.

Parents should not ask their small children for advice or what their child wants to do for the day because the area of making plans and decisions is reserved only for the parents. Parents should not ask their small child for approval after making plans or decisions by asking, "Is that okay?" In time and with some rebellion, the plans or decisions are not okay, and there will be confrontation and arguments over what has been decided. I think in this way we train our children to tell us their selfish plans against the loving plan that benefits everyone. Parents have confidence in their decision-making ability to make the right choices, and they don't need approval for their decisions from their small children. Of course the parent will make some of those plans and decisions based upon the child's likes and dislikes.

Make the Plan and Follow It

It is the parent who outlines the day with a plan and then follows through to see that those plans happen as much as possible. The plan may be to go to Grandma's house, then go shopping, and then come back home to do some chores and get dinner ready. Plans, decisions, and goals are made every day for many things, for work, for activities, and for fun. Plans are made for the day, for the week, and sometimes much further out in time. The child is consistently told what the plan is and what will happen next.

When plans are followed with little change, then the child knows what to expect and what to prepare for. Sometimes plans for the child make a lot of work for the parent, but when children are raised this way, they come to trust their parents' choices for them and are more secure in their little personalities. Children trust the loving decisions and plans you make for them, no matter what else happens. The plans you make for your small children give them anticipation and hope. You create hope and expectation in your small children by the plans you make for them. They gain important experience at a very young age by seeing and following the many loving choices and decisions their parents have made for them.

As children get a little older, the parent lets them make some choices and decisions for themselves. Do you want to wear the red top or the blue one today? They are given simple and easy choices at first. By the time they get even older, they have a long record of the many good choices you have made for them. Try to guess what all this will do in a child who grows up this way. Older children may never admit it, but they will make their own choices based on what they have learned from you. All the decisions you made for them when they were small will flavor many of their decisions for the rest of their lives.

Just imagine a home where no plans are made or where plans that are made are suddenly and constantly changed or canceled. Crises are a constant companion to children in those situations. Children raised in this way do not know what to expect or what to prepare for. Instead they learn disappointment, disorder, frustration, and insecurity. Usually children in homes like this are permitted to make their own decisions way too early in life, and far too many mistakes are made. Children in homes like this often go astray and follow their parents' poor examples.

Children raised in a home where plans and decisions are made and followed learn to trust in their parents' loving decisions. That ability to trust their parents' decisions gives them a better chance at trusting in the Lord. That trust in their parents carries over into their faith in the Lord. You make it easier for your children to trust God when they trust you by all the loving plans and decisions you have made for them.

God, the Loving Parent of His Children

I believe that God is like the loving parent who does not just make plans for us, but He knows our future and tells us about it through prophecy. God totally accepts us no matter what kind of home we were raised in. God becomes our loving parent. He outlines our future by prophecy so we will know what to expect and what to prepare for. God has plans for us, and He makes decisions for us based upon His righteousness. He keeps a vision before us so we can be secure in our faith and in Him.

Remember how much of the Bible is about prophecy? Twenty seven percent! I think the Lord really wants us to know what will happen. Prophecy is God's way of preparing His children for what is coming and to draw all His children into relationship. That is right and good for the Lord to do for His children. The area of making plans is only for the parent; the area of telling us the future is God's alone. We know the future because we know the Lord; we know His plans and His prophecies that give us vision, direction, and many more benefits, and what is wrong with that? Please understand that God wants us to have a vision. Having a vision benefits us. A vision is for future things, like the promised Messiah. If a vision is for future things, then we only know about those future things through prophecy. Having a vision helps our faith by giving us hope. God loves us and always wants the best for us. When we know what will happen, it makes us secure in the one who knows all things.

Just a word to parents who have small children. If you want to be the wise and good parent pictured here, you can begin today by making all the plans and decisions for your own small children. Proverbs 22:6 says, "Train up a child in the way he should go: and when he is old he will not depart from it." I think a part of training up children in the way that they should go is to make all of those plans and decisions for them so that those plans and decisions you have made will flavor your children's decisions for the rest of their lives.

I have seen big, strong young men with their small children; they are bent way over, inclining their ear to a child, asking him or her what he or she wants to do, and the child, of course, is telling him. This big, strong father has given the decision- and plan-making authority over to a two-year-old. We must not be afraid to make plans that lovingly benefit our small children, nor think that we must reward children to prevent bad behavior. It should be commonplace to have children follow what the parents have decided for them.

Now I don't deny that there are strong-willed children who will challenge you in every step of the way. Strong-willed children may be leaders in the making, but don't engage it when they challenge you. Lovingly and firmly confront it when it is appropriate. The result of all this effort is to give your child experience in trusting and following, two very valuable traits in serving God. Your children will grow up with an ability, even a propensity, to follow the Lord. The way in which you bring up your children will directly affect their ability to commit to the Lord. This is not to say that will never learn how to lead; that comes from within the child and is something that God will put in his or her heart to glorify Him.

CHAPTER 11

Can We Know God's Purpose for Prophecy?

Some may say I am being presumptuous when I speak on God's purpose for prophecy. It may be said that we can't know God's purpose for prophecy because we can't know the mind of God because "His ways are past finding out," as it says in Romans 11:33. Or they may misquote 1 Corinthians 2:16, saying, "For who hath known the mind of the Lord ...?" It seems logical to say, "We can't know what God is up to." While I'm aware that His ways are past finding out, I can say with full assurance that there are things that God wants us to not merely to know about Him, as wonderful as that is, but to know Him personally and what He is doing. God has told us of His desires for many things, including worship. "But the hour cometh and now is, when the true worshippers shall worship the Father in spirit and in truth: for the Father seeketh such to worship him" (John 4:23). God wants us to believe in Him, as it says, "For God so loved the world, that he gave his only begotten Son, that whosoever believeth in him should not perish, but have everlasting life" (John 3:16).

He wants to reward those who diligently seek Him, as Hebrews 11:6 says, "But without faith is impossible to please him: for he that cometh to God must believe that he is and he is a rewarder of them that diligently seek him." These verses and many, many more show us God's heart, what He wants, and what pleases Him. Certainly God is not unknowable. He wants us to know Him and to be with Him forever. We can see this is very evident in the Scriptures.

Ye are my friends, if ye do whatsoever I command you. Henceforth I call you not servants; for the servant knoweth not what his lord doeth: but I have called you friends; for all things that I have heard of my Father I have made known unto you. (John 15:14–16)

There are more Scriptures to rely on in God's Word to see His purpose for prophecy, as we are about to explain. It is important to know the Lord and know what He is about to do. Prophecy lets us know what God is about to do, as Amos 3:7 tells us, "Surely the Lord God will do nothing, but he revealeth his secret unto his servants the prophets." There is an everlasting punishment for doing things in the name of the Lord but not knowing Him, as Matthew 7:21–23 shows us. Jesus said he would profess to them, "I never knew you: Depart from me, ye that work iniquity." I'm sure that none of us want to hear those words spoken to us on that day.

The Bible certainly is many things. It is an instruction manual on life, it is a lamp for our path, and it is God's Word. I look at the Bible as those things too, but I also look at it to tell me how to have closeness with God in an active relationship. It shows me His great love, and that makes me want to respond in kind to Him. God wants us to know Him. Just look at all the pages in your Bible that tell us about Him and how He has interacted with all different kinds of people in many situations as examples to learn from. He gave us the Bible as a sort of love letter to explain so many things about Him. The process of reading the Bible is more than just accumulating information about God, ancient history, and some good moral lessons. It tells us who He is, what He likes, and what He does not like and how we can properly respond and have a relationship with Him. It is essential to change because of its words, but if we stop there, we fail, because the Lord wants us to know Him through His Word. I believe God's greatest desire is to make a strong connection with us in a close relationship.

And they shall teach no more every man his neighbor, and every man his brother, saying Know the Lord: for they shall all know me, from the least of them unto the greatest of them, saith the Lord: for I will forgive their iniquity, and I will remember their sin no more. (Jer. 31:34)

At that time Jesus answered and said, I thank thee, O Father, Lord of heaven and earth, because thou hast hid these things from the wise and prudent, and revealed them unto babes. Even so, Father: for so it seemed good in thy sight. All things are delivered unto me of my Father: and no man knoweth the Son, but the Father; neither knoweth any man the Father, save the Son, and he to whomsoever the Son will reveal him. (Matt. 11:25–27)

And this is life eternal, that they might know thee the only true God, and Jesus Christ whom thou hast sent. (John 17:3)

And we know that the Son of God is come, and hath given us an understanding, that we may know him that is true, even his Son Jesus Christ, This is the true God, and eternal life. (1 John 5:20)

Faith-Based Relationship

For most Christians, having a relationship with someone you can see is difficult enough. We often make mistakes that violate our relationships with people. Our relationship with the Lord is much different than with people because we have to have faith to believe that God is real. Being in relationship with someone you can't see is more difficult. There is no element of faith in our relationships with people, who can see and hear and touch, but faith enters into our relationship with God because we can't see Him.

Remember what Hebrews 11:6 says: "But without faith it is impossible

to please him: for he that cometh to God must believe that he is ..."
That is a much different way of having relationship than what we are
used to. Being in a relationship with the Almighty is a relationship like
no other we have experienced before. There are new relational rules
to learn, and there is a difference in the way we interact with Him to
hear His voice. We experience the still, silent voice in a much different
way than we hear our friend's voice. In a way, we have to learn a whole
new way of interacting in our relationship with God to make this new
faith-based relationship work.

Some Christians do not read their Bibles and yet say they know the
Lord. That should be a cause for great concern. That's like watching
someone on TV with the sound turned off. The person on the TV is
talking about his life, what he likes, where he lives, his job, his history,
and his contact information, but you have the sound tuned off, so you
can't hear a single thing he is saying. You miss all the details of his life.
You wouldn't learn anything about him, and thus you would have a hard
time knowing and understanding him. Many people know about God,
but the way we know God in a personal way is through His word, in
prayer, and with a servant's heart through the guidance of the Holy
Spirit. "Thy word is thy lamp unto my feet, and a light unto my path"
(Ps. 119:105).

Yes, we can know God's purpose for prophecy but more than that, He
wants us to know it because He loves us and wants to bless us with its
benefits. All Scripture, including Bible prophecy, helps us to know His
loving nature and His loving kindness, faithfulness, and desire to be
close to us. We respond to His desire to have closeness with Him in a
relationship that is like no other. So yes, we can know God's purpose
for prophecy because knowing it helps us see His loving nature and
His desire to be close to us.

CHAPTER 12

The Purpose for Prophecy

By now it is obvious that the purpose for prophecy has leaked out in previous chapters. It is no secret. The things God does are no secret to His children, and it is the same in this book. Now I don't deny that prophecy has many benefits and functions, but it has one main purpose. Prophecy has that quality about it that wonderfully colors just about every facet of our faith. Obviously it tells us the future. It has detailed battle plans; it started some kind of preparation for something coming in the future, such as building an ark or storing grain. It reaches into us and prepares our hearts to be with God by repentance, and at the same time it creates hope and glorifies God. The coming of the Messiah began as prophecy. Many Bible stories have a prophecy as their beginning and/or basis of the story. Without the prophecy, the Bible stories we know and love change and become much different than we know them or they would've never happened at all.

The entire New Testament is loaded with the fulfillment of over one hundred messianic prophecies rooted in the Old Testament to prove that Jesus is the Messiah. Some of those prophecies were spoken over nineteen hundred years before Jesus was born. Without prophetic fulfillment of those Messianic prophecies, our understanding of the New Testament and our perception of Jesus change drastically. The entire story about the Jews being in Egypt was one soaked in prophecy. The reason the Jews even knew about the Promised Land was because of prophecy. Prophecy has foretold the destruction of the temple, Jesus' return, and

Peter's denials. By prophecy we know of the benefits we will receive in heaven. Take all prophecy from the Bible and our Bible, our faith, and our history would look much different.

There is a saying, because of these very old prophecies being fulfilled in the New Testament, that says, "The Old Testament is the New Testament concealed, and the New Testament is the Old Testament revealed." Of course there were many prophecies that were prophesied and fulfilled in the Old Testament. The Old Testament prophecies about the Messiah were somewhat hidden in their meanings, and they so confused the ancient Jews. Was the Messiah going to come from Bethlehem, from Nazareth, or from Egypt? Oh the arguments they must've had among themselves.

Many of the Old Testament prophecies about the Messiah were revealed in their New Testament fulfillment by Jesus. We are no different in our varying views of prophecy today. End-times prophecies somewhat confuse us, and at times we have difficulty agreeing on the prophecies that are going to happen next, the order of things that will happen, or if any more fulfillments will ever happen again. It is only because of our position in history that we can see that the arguments of the ancient Jews about the Messiah were too narrow in their views causing the arguments. We can rightfully say that the Old Testament is the New Testament concealed and the New Testament is the Old Testament revealed because we can see how all that happened. The only way we can see it is because we understand the differing Messianic prophecies were all fulfilled in Jesus.

There are many views and opinions about prophecy. Some interpretations and applications are good and some are not so good, but understanding God's purpose for it has been missing for a long time, and the church misses out on all its benefits. We've been fixated on one side of the coin for so long. Let's turn that coin over and try to see what the other side of the coin looks like. Verses that are prophetic fill over a quarter of all the verses in our Bible, and we must know the purpose God intended for so much prophecy in the Bible. We know that the writers of books on prophecy have done their job of interpreting and applying with the intent to warn us of what is coming; now we must see God's purpose for prophecy.

Many books have been written to help us in our understanding of the Bible. These books are called commentaries. When we read other people's opinions about the Scriptures, we can better make up our own minds about what we believe. It is like having expert advisors to help us make up our minds about what we believe. Our own pastor, minister, or priest helps us to make decisions about what we believe. Did you know that the Bible itself contains its very own commentary? There are some verses that offer comments on some other part of Scriptures that can give definition, legitimacy, and function to those Scriptures. Daniel 9:2 records that the prophet Daniel read his predecessor Jeremiah's words. Whenever Jesus in the New Testament quotes a prophet from the Old Testament, it lends credibility to that prophet's words that they are from God. The Bible has some comments on prophecy too; it gives us a look at prophecy that helps us to understand the purpose of prophecy.

There is one commentary of prophecy in Amos that is very telling about the way the Lord does things. Amos 3:7 says, "Surely the Lord God will do nothing, but he revealeth his secret unto his servants the prophets." Another way to say this is to say, "Surely the Lord God will never do anything without first revealing what He will do to His servants the prophets" (author's paraphrase).

What have we just read? The Lord never does anything until He has first revealed what He is going to do to the prophets. First God tells the prophets what He will do, and then He does it. Of course God created the heavens and the earth without telling any prophet because those things were done before man was created. If we want to know what God is going to do, we study what the prophets have said.

God has a special relationship with His servants the prophets to let His people know what He will do. Please understand that God first tells the prophets what He is going to do and then He does it, and all of that is done with a purpose. What is the purpose behind God saying what He will do and then doing it? It is to show His faithfulness and provide us with a volume of testimonies to His faithfulness, which also glorifies Him. Faithfulness is demonstrated by doing what you have said you will do. It is the same with God; His faithfulness is shown by what He says and by what He does to honor His own words.

The testimonies of God's faithfulness create trust and relationship with the Lord. We react and interact with prophecy from our hearts where the work of the Holy Spirit is done to bring us close to the Lord. We are supposed to interact with prophecy. Prophecy is for our benefit. The four elements of prophecy come into play here. It is through the process of the four elements of prophecy that prophecy becomes interactive because it creates a response to prophetic fulfillment. God's interactive nature is served by prophecy to prove and glorify Him to us so we are drawn to Him in faith and trust. Can we say this is true of all Bible prophecy? Yes, it is true every time, in every prophecy.

If you look at all Bible prophecy, you will see that God first speaks the word about the future, and then it comes true. Sometimes that word is about Him doing something and then He performs His word. Prophecy is one of the ways God interacts with the world for the purpose of proving Himself. First He says what He will do and then does it. Amos 3:7 is the way the Lord does things and is a part of His purpose for prophecy, the way in which He does things clearly shows His faithfulness and His power to bring to pass the words that He has spoken.

Please understand that God wants to prove Himself to you so that you will believe in Him. Notice that whenever there is a proving circumstance in the Bible, God always shows up. We can see the story of Daniel and the dream that the king had and Daniel's prayer asking that God would reveal the dream and the meaning (Dan. 2:1–45). Daniel's three friends who wouldn't bow down to the king's idol and said that God would deliver them from the fiery furnace are another good example of this (Dan. 3:1–30). God has proven Himself time after time, from the priests carrying the ark about to step into the Jordan River (Josh. 3:8–17), to asking us to prove Him when we tithe (Mal. 3:10), and Elijah on Mt. Carmel with the 950 prophets of Baal and Ashera. He proves He alone is God by the glory of the heavens (Ps. 19:1) and in the amazing way in which we were made (Ps. 139:14), but there is even more of this proving in prophecy.

There is another situation where God gave someone the ability to prove Him. What did Moses say to God at the burning bush? Moses said the people of Israel wouldn't believe that God had sent him to them. God tells him His name, and Moses further doubts that anyone will believe God has sent him. God transformed the rod Moses had into a serpent and also told Moses to put his hand into his bosom (under his clothes into his chest). It came out as white as snow, he put it back into his chest, and it came out normal, like his other hand. Why did God give this ability of the rod turning into a snake and making his hand white with leprosy? God gave Moses the ability to do these supernatural things to prove that he was sent by God. God wanted Moses to have proof that he spoke for God. There was some prophecy involved here, but understand that God was giving Moses things to prove he was sent by God to deliver the people from their bondage in Egypt.

"Thy word is true from the beginning: and every one of thy righteous judgments endureth forever" (Ps. 119:160).

That Ye May Believe

There is another short commentary-type verse in John's gospel that helps to give a defining role to the purpose of prophecy. It's just a short verse and easily overlooked. Jesus is speaking in this commentary in John

13:19. He says; "Now I tell you before it comes, that when it comes to pass you may believe that I am *he*." Jesus repeats this saying in John 14:29 and somewhat again in John 16:4.

What is Jesus saying by this comment on His own words? First He is saying that He is God because He is speaking the future on His own authority. The first part of that verse says, "Behold I tell you before it come." It says that Jesus has knowledge of the future. Only God knows the future. He is proving He is God by telling us the future by Himself, not because He is inspired to speak or because He is speaking on behalf of the Lord like all the prophets did before Him. Jesus is speaking the future on His own authority because He spoke as God because He is God. The second part of that verse says, "That, when it is come to pass ye may believe that I am he." This shows us the reason, indeed the purpose, for all prophecy from Jesus. That purpose for telling us the future is so we will believe in Him.

Knowing the future is very special. There are many pretenders who say they know the future, but only God knows the future completely. God has designed the use of prophecy to not only tell us about the future, but by using prophecy and fulfillment, He proves Himself to us. God not only knows the future completely, but He also tells us about it to prove who He is to us so we will come to Him and know Him. By prophecy God proves Himself to us by doing something we are incapable of doing so we will know He exists, believe in Him, and love Him above all else. The result of all this is relationship. God wants us to respond to prophetic fulfillment in a faith that starts relationship.

The word *believe* in John 13:19 has a dual meaning from the Greek that not only means to have faith, but it also means "to trust." Jesus tells us the future before it comes so that we will decide to have faith in Him. We can't have faith in something we don't believe exists or in someone we can't trust, so the Lord provides proof after proof by prophecy after prophecy of His existence for the express purpose of creating relationship with you.

Prophecy's Proving Ground of Fulfillment

There is a new bridge in my town that spans an interstate highway. The tall columns of reinforced concrete of support that hold up the bridge are very far apart—so far apart that they seem to be unable to support the weight of not only the bridge but the traffic on the bridge. I don't like crossing that bridge because I don't see how it is strong enough to support the weight demanded of it, especially the span in the middle of those supports. The surface of the bridge is not smooth like a new bridge should be; there is some sagging between the concrete seams so there is an up-and-down motion one feels while driving across the bridge. That rough ride on a new bridge adds to my apprehension when I'm driving on it. I admit that more than once I have gone around that bridge because I don't trust it. I think that some morning I'll open the newspaper and see a picture of twisted steel and crumbled concrete collapsed on the interstate and a headline that says, 'Bridge Collapses onto Interstate," with an accompanying sub-headline that says, "Engineers baffled by bridge collapse." Well, I won't be baffled at all. I'll know why it fell down; those supports were way too far apart!

All praise to God because He is not like that bridge, because He has provided so many proofs that support His testimonies so that we can trust in Him. Faith and trust, no matter how small at first, are the initial steps that start a relationship with God. Faith is the twin sister of trust. When God proves Himself by Bible prophecy, we move toward Him in faith and trust, and the result is relationship. We don't trust strangers with our credit card numbers and other personal information; we only trust those who prove themselves worthy of our trust. God is more worthy of our faith and trust than any person. Trust and faith are the building blocks of relationship.

God is in a position of constantly proving Himself to all generations from the time of Adam and Eve to today. Just name one Bible character who didn't know and experience or speak prophecy. Please understand that most of the Bible was written by prophets. Everyone in the Bible knew about prophecy, and they all knew that true prophecy came only from God. They knew that He proves Himself by prophetic fulfillment to them because they couldn't see Him, so He gave them prophecy to prove He is real, to prove that He is almighty God. He gives us the whole Bible record of prophecy and their fulfillments to prove His existence so that we can come to Him and know Him.

Remember that Jesus said that when it is come to pass, you may believe? It is by fulfilled prophecy that faith is created. The end-times prophecies are not fulfilled prophecy—not yet anyway—so they don't prove God exists. End-times prophecies warn us of what is coming, but the last-days prophecies are not something we place our hope in. Certainly the inheritance we will receive according to the promises of God are not fulfilled yet either, but unlike end-times prophecies, the prophecy/promises of our inheritance is where we derive so much of our hope in Christ and that is a sustainer of our faith.

Hebrews 11:6 says this too: "But without faith it is impossible to please him: for he that cometh to God must believe that he is and that he is a rewarder of them that diligently seek him" God proves He alone is God by creation and by prophecy and fulfillment. God draws us into relationship by prophecy. Prophecy proves that He is, and once we believe that He exists, we learn that God is a rewarder of those who diligently seek Him out. Prophecy is an essential part of our faith, created and put there by God to build our trust in Him. What is the most important reward God gives to those who diligently seek Him? Relationship with the Almighty!

God does something we cannot do, that is to tell us the future so that upon seeing the fulfillment, we will know that He exists and will be drawn into relationship with Him. The result is relationship. This is the purpose of all Bible prophecy—to draw everyone into relationship. Just as the prophecy through Jonah drew an entire city into relationship with God, God desires over a quarter of His Word to have that same effect upon the whole world.

We have another one of those commentaries-type verses in John 16:4 where Jesus says, "But these things I have told you, that when the time shall come, ye may remember that I told you of them ..." Jesus was commenting on His own words again and telling His disciples why He was telling them the future. The reason Jesus was telling His disciples the future was so when they saw fulfillment they would remember that Jesus first told them it would happen. God tells us something will happen, and then we see it come to be fulfilled and remember that He first told us that it would happen. Then we believe in Him. When the time of fulfillment came, the disciples would remember that Jesus first told them it would happen. Then they would believe in Him as God and have relationship. We hear Him speak it and remember it when it comes to pass. It is then, when we see it come to pass or be fulfilled, that we know God has just proven Himself to us. I believe the ancient Jews knew something about prophecy that we don't know today.

Remember that there is a difference in the way the prophets spoke for God and the way Jesus spoke as God. Jesus never said, "Thus saith the Lord," before speaking prophecy; He spoke it on His own authority because He is God. The Jews of Jesus' time understood that to speak prophecy without first saying, "Thus saith the Lord" was to say that the person speaking on his own authority was God almighty or a deceiver. In Matthew 26:62–65, Jesus has been arrested and is standing before the council and the high priest. The high priest accuses Jesus, and Jesus answers him and prophesies: "And Jesus saith unto him, Thou hast said: nevertheless I say unto you, Hereafter shall ye see the Son of man sitting on the right hand of power, and coming in the clouds of heaven." What was the reaction to Jesus' prophecy that He spoke on

His own authority? Verse 65 says, "Then the high priest rent [tore] his clothes, saying, He hath spoken blasphemy; what further proof need have we of witnesses? Behold, now ye have heard his blasphemy." The high priest called it blasphemy when Jesus told him the future on His own authority.

In the proving process of prophecy and fulfillment God is seeking you to be in relationship with Him. Why did God fill over a quarter of His Word with prophecy? He did give us proof after proof after proof to build a strong trust in our hearts for Him. The Lord filled much of His Word with about a thousand prophecies to create and deepen relationship with you. Over a quarter of the Word of God is prophecy—an overwhelming flood of proof that He wants relationship with you. When we with open and seeking hearts see God prove Himself to us time after time by prophecy and fulfillment after prophecy and fulfillment, we are left with the wonderfully indelible mark of faith.

The forty-eighth chapter of Isaiah is a wonderful chapter in the Bible containing another one of those in-the-Bible commentaries. The Jews are worshipping idols and false gods, and God is pleading with Israel, saying that He alone is worthy of their faith and not their idols. In Isaiah 48:3–6 God comments on the prophecies that He has spoken to them:

> I have declared the former things from the beginning; and they went forth out of my mouth, and I shewed them; I did them suddenly, and they came to pass. Because I know that thou art obstinate, and thy neck is an iron sinew, and thy brow brass; I have even from the beginning declared it to thee; before it came to pass I shewed it to thee: lest thou shouldest say, Mine idol hath done them, and my graven image, and my molten image, hath commanded them. Thou hast heard, see all this; and will not ye declare it? I have shewed thee

new things from this time, even hidden things, and thou didst not know them.

God is telling the Jews in that section of Scripture that He has proved who He is to them by telling them the future by prophecy. God has proven Himself worthy, yet they hardened their hearts to say their idols did what the Lord had done. The Lord is scolding the Jews in these verses out of Isaiah, using prophecy to show them that their idols didn't foretell the future; God did. They just didn't want to see that it was God who was proving Himself to them because their sin felt good, and they didn't want to change what fed their flesh and not their spirit. It was true then, and today people are no different. Anyone unwilling to change will take what God has done to fulfill His own Word and call it coincidence or foolishness. They don't want the multitude of proofs God has given them and out of their bloated egos demand proof from God on their own terms. God proves He alone is worthy of our trust and faith in Him time after time.

Why So Much Proof?

Why does God have to prove Himself to us so many times by prophecy in the Bible? Sometimes I think we just don't get it. There may be a very good reason why the Scriptures call us sheep, because we are so dumb. In the above verse from Isaiah, God calls the Jews obstinate, with an iron neck that will not bow to Him and a brow that is brass that will not listen to Him. We are not any different than those ancient people. We are so used to seeing and dealing with the everyday physical things that we can see; we're just not experienced in the multitude of spiritual things God is doing for our benefit. I think that when we get to heaven, God will make us aware of all the testimonies and proofs that He placed before us while we were still here on the earth. By these proofs He will show us all the times He was working strongly on our behalf and we doubted Him. We just didn't see it or understand it here on earth. It will not be for the purpose of condemning us but to show His great faithfulness and love for us. We didn't see these proofs because of our unbelief or because we were unlearned and unskilled in the spiritual.

Most of the time we are ignorant of what God has done or what He is doing right now. We don't often look up and see the stars and the sunsets and know that the heavens declare the glory of God, as it says in Psalm 19:1. We don't look at the intricate way our bodies were made and see the design of God present in our bodies, as it says in Psalm 139:14. When we look at ourselves, we tend to see all the flaws in the way we were made because we compare ourselves to a false image of what we think we should look like. Proverbs 16:7 says, "When a man's ways please the Lord, he maketh even his enemies to be at peace with him." This verse shows that God moves in ways that I cannot see for my benefit, not only to make my enemies to be at peace with me but for many other things for my benefit. I think God knows we are feeble and we don't often see Him in His creation, and He offers even more proof of who He is and that is shown through prophecy.

Did God have a purpose to sending the Son to die on a cross? Of course! That purpose is displayed in John 3:16 and it reads in part, "Whosoever believeth on him should not perish, but have everlasting life." Please understand that God's purpose for sending Jesus is so that we will have everlasting life with God in heaven in close relationship. The purpose for eternal life is for eternal fellowship with the Lord. The purpose for prophecy is exactly the same. So that we will repent, have faith, and be drawn into relationship with God and have everlasting life—an everlasting relationship and an everlasting closeness with God in heaven. There is no difference in God's purpose for the cross and God's purpose for prophecy. They are both meant to create and deepen relationship with Him.

Remember the four elements of prophecy? The first three elements of prophecy are first to hear the prophecy, second to wait and watch for it, and third to see its fulfillment. The fourth element of prophecy, as mentioned before, is the most important element because of what it does inside us. This is what the purpose for prophecy is all about—the reason why prophecy exists. I believe it is the reason why God includes so much prophecy in His Word. When I see something come true that was first foretold, it changes me; I can't be the same inside. I am drawn to the one who has proven He is real by telling me the future. An understanding of biblical prophecy draws us to faith in Jesus. Therefore, prophecy is like God's own evangelism to us and to the world. He is reaching out to us to create faith and trust. In Matthew 28:16–20, we find the verses we call the great commission. It reads in part, "Go ye therefore, and teach all nations, baptizing them in the name of the Father, and of the Son, and of the Holy Ghost." God wants us, once we are saved and serving Him, to go out and teach others about Him so others will know Him too.

Is That a Fulfillment?

When non-Christians see a prophecy fulfilled, they go through some changes. It produces either faith or denial. God has just proven Himself with prophetic fulfillment. Fulfilled prophecy proves that God is real. Now a decision has to be made. Do you follow the one who knows the future, or do you deny it, condemn it, and go on and do your own thing for the rest of your life? If the choice is to believe and follow God, then you must change because the Lord who has foretold and fulfilled His words has also specified a way of life for you to live in order to obtain His promises for you. Everything in life has to change if you are to be in a close relationship with the one who knows the future. Now there has to be repentance from sin and a willingness to submit your life to Him and obey other words He has spoken to you in His Word.

I often wonder how many people in Egypt started believing in the true God because of the interpretation of Pharaoh's prophetic dream that God gave to Joseph. That single interpretation of a dream saved the whole nation of Egypt. Certainly most people in Egypt must've known that a Hebrew felon from prison saved the nation of not only Egypt but the surrounding nations from famine. Yes, the Bible acknowledges that Joseph came to realize that God had a purpose in bringing him and his family into Egypt, but the Bible doesn't go into all the faith that the interpretation of Pharaoh's dream must have created in the hearts of the Egyptian people.

I think that is true again 430 years later when the Jews left Egypt. During the ten plagues of Egypt, there must've been Egyptians saying in their hearts, "Our gods are nothing, but the God of the Jews, He is God!" Maybe faith was birthed in their hearts as they watched the miracles God did in their midst. Egypt was a world power and a destination of travelers and businessmen from the rest of the world. Maybe some of those travelers and businessmen saw the miracles God did to free the Hebrew slaves and they too decided to have faith. It is possible that they brought back news of what God did in Egypt to their own land, and that news started faith there too. The Jews may've left Egypt when the Exodus began, but faith in God may've been left in the hearts of the Egyptians after seeing all the miracles God did to deliver the Jews from their bondage.

God reaches out to us to draw us into relationship with Him by prophecy, and that is the most important element. It is the purpose for prophecy, the relationship it creates. God does miracles in the sight of many people not mentioned in the Bible, and those miracles may draw people on the sidelines of the Bible stories to faith in the Lord. God uses biblical prophecy not only to draw you into relationship with Him, but He continually proves Himself within our relationship.

Some people have known that God has proven who He is to them, but they enjoy their sin too much to change. We see this throughout the Word, and we see it around us today. They look for reasons not to change and not serve God. In some people, the dread of change makes them deny that God has fulfilled His words. They will say that a prophetic fulfillment is just a coincidence and not something God foretold. They can live with themselves easier when they tell themselves that and try hard to believe it. It is too easy for them to classify religious people as hypocrites. They can't be religious because then they will become hypocrites too. But the underlying motivator not to accept Jesus is that they would lose the sin they love so much. The excuses they use in their decision to not follow Jesus are their own choice, and one choice has very extreme eternal consequences.

When people of faith see prophecy fulfilled, their faith is deepened, enriched, and strengthened. Ancient people experienced it, and we stand in awe of it today. We see a prophecy fulfilled that is seven hundred years old, like the prophecy from Isaiah 7:14, where we learn of a virgin who will conceive a son. We stand speechless, seeing God fulfill His words time after time. Seeing prophecy fulfilled affirms our hope in Christ. It makes us feel secure in the Lord because He is so faithful and able to keep even the least of the words He speaks. We come to understand that God knows what He is doing and everything that will happen.

But I Already Believe—Why Do I Need Proof?

You may say, "I already believe in God and in what Jesus did on the cross to die for may sin so I can be forgiven of my sin and be free and redeemed." While you are free in Christ and are forgiven, you need reminders of what God has done for you. The Bible repeats something over 180 times to people of faith. Remember that after the children of Israel came out of their bondage in Egypt, they are reminded by God over 180 times what God did to deliver them out of their bondage. As we have mentioned before, these reminders go on to remind them about their wanderings in the desert and crossing the Jordan and going on to conquer the Promised Land. Did they need those reminders? God thought they did, and He put those reminders into His Word that many times. Remember that God did that, as we discussed before, to remind them of His love for them. They needed that, and you do too.

Remember all the feasts God commanded the Jews to have as a reminder of what God did for them. Ten feasts of Israel celebrate what God did to help the Jews and to remind them of what He did for them. A loving God gave us all of these reminders of Egypt, including having the feasts, to remind us of His love for us. Do you want God reminding you of His great love for you? Of course you do; it is His way of loving on you. Are you thinking that you already believe in God and you don't need all that proof that prophetic fulfillment stuff? Then I would say to look at the reminders of Egypt and the reminders that all the feasts bring to the Jews and know that you need reminders too.

If you are a parent, you remind your children of how much you do for them, not to nag them but to prove your love for them by all that you do for them. As shown before, all these reminders show your love for your children. God does this for us too and shows His love for us. If you already believe, then accept the proof as a way of reminding you of why you believe. Remember Egypt. Remember the feasts. Remember the proof lest you forget. Let the reminders of His love wash over you with regularity. Soak it all up like a sponge, and accept His great love.

Everything that God does, every expression of God, every word of God has the express purpose of creating and deepening relationship with you. Why did Jesus die on the cross to take away our sins? Again, why? Jesus died to remove that one thing that blocks our relationship with God. Why did the Father send the Son into the world? Yes, so the Son could redeem mankind from sin and death for the purpose of fellowship.

You may already be familiar with Proverbs 3:5, which says, "Trust in the Lord with all thine heart and lean not unto thine own understanding. In all thy ways acknowledge Him and He shall direct thy paths." You've probably heard this verse quoted many times, but in understanding God's use of prophecy to reach out to His creation to create relationship, do you see that this verse is all about relationship? The interactive nature of trust and direction is relationship. We get to hear the Lord's direction when we trust in Him with all our hearts. We come to that point of trusting in the Lord with all our hearts through understanding all the proofs of His love that God present to us, much of it through fulfilled Bible prophecy. You could say that the Lord has helped us to trust in Him with all our hearts by offering us great proof of who He is because He always keeps His word.

Oh what a huge depth of security there is that comes from prophecy that creates a strong trust for the almighty God, who can fulfill His words whether they come hundreds or even thousands of years after they were spoken! We all pray as believers, asking God to bring us closer to Him. Prophecy has already been prescribed by our Great Physician to give us proofs of why we can trust Him in ever-increasing ways. Prophecy is often the venue in which the faithfulness of God is displayed. When God says it and then fulfills it, we see His faithfulness. Time after time as His faithfulness is displayed in the Word, it helps us to trust Him. We are drawn to trust Him in ever-increasing ways because He keeps proving Himself. Our faith grows deeper and deeper. Our joy grows as we rejoice over what He has done because God almighty is glorified. We rejoice in the same way Simeon and Anna did when they saw Jesus, and they knew by the Holy Spirit that this young child was the long-promised Messiah. So prophecy is not only for creating faith; it is also for strengthening our faith.

The Greatest Commandments

In Matthew 22:35–40 Jesus was asked, "What is the greatest commandment in the law?" Jesus responded by quoting Deuteronomy 6:5, saying, "You shall love the Lord your God with all your heart, with all your soul and with all your strength." Then Jesus offered a further commentary of the law by identifying another commandment as the second greatest commandment that is like unto the first, quoting a part of Leviticus 19:18, which says in full, "You shall not avenge, nor bear any grudges against the children of your people, but you shall love your neighbor as yourself; I am the Lord." Jesus commented on the importance of these two verses by saying in Matthew 22:40, "On these two commandments hang all the law and the prophets."

These two smallish verses repeated in the Bible in only a couple of other places are so important. What are the two greatest commandments all about? Well, very simply they are about love and relationships. The first one shows us to put God first; the second one shows us to put a value on our neighbors equal to us. When Jesus referred to the law in verse 40, He was referring to the first five books of the Bible (Torah) written by the lawgiver Moses. These two greatest commandments are not a part of the Ten Commandments, and we know that there were many other laws in the Old Testament that the Jews followed, for a total list of the 613 commandments or Mitzvot. Jesus says that those two commandments were greater than all the rest.

Now remember that Jesus said upon these two commandments hang all the law and the prophets. I can understand if Jesus said upon these two commandments hang all the law because both of these commandments were in the law of Moses, but why did He say "and the prophets"? The prophets' writings were a completely different portion of Scripture. I think He said it because if we understand that the law showed us we were in sin and what He expects of us, then prophets and their prophecies proved God was God. These two go hand in hand to work for our faith.

In Galatians 3:24 there is another one of those in-the-Bible-commentaries and it says, "Wherefore the law was our schoolmaster to bring us to Christ that we might be justified through faith." The law brings us to Christ, and through the prophets, God proves Himself to us, jumpstarting trust. Prophecy was on a level of importance with the Law of Moses. Jesus was implying two things when He tied those two commandments to the law and the prophets. First, the law told us what sin was, and by that sin came death. Second, the prophecies from God spoken by the mouths of the prophets were proven to be from God by fulfillment. They proved that He was real and knew things about the future that people couldn't know. The law was fulfilled by a perfect sacrifice by He who knew no sin. Speaking of Jesus in 2 Corinthians 5:21, Paul says, "For he hath made him to be sin for us, who knew no sin; that we might be made the righteousness of God in him" Jesus knew no sin but became sin on the cross for us.

Jesus said something that is related to what He said in the above verse. He identified the two greatest commandments above, and both those commandments are related to Matthew 5:18 where Jesus says He had not come to destroy the law and the prophets but to fulfill them. Jesus came with a purpose for the law and the prophets. He came to redeem man under the law by first being approved that He alone was worthy to do that by fulfilling prophecy. In other words, Jesus first got the official redemption credentials by fulfilling over one hundred Old Testament Messianic prophecies concerning Him, which gave Him alone the title of Messiah. He also lived a perfect life as a "lamb without spot" (1 Peter 1:19) to redeem man from the law of sin and death by the cross. Remember, living under the law said that you could only offer up a perfect lamb for sacrifice for sin. He fulfilled one part and redeemed with the other. Proven worthy, granted authority, bore our sin, and gave Himself once and for all a sacrifice for sin, according to the law, to redeem mankind from the grip of sin and death. He spoke the future, He fulfilled the past, He lived with the knowledge of all things, and He was our perfect sacrifice.

Indeed the law was our schoolmaster (teacher) to bring us to Christ so we might be justified by faith in Jesus' work on the cross, but the thing that pre-qualifies Jesus as the one who justifies us before God is in the undeniable and overwhelming multitude of fulfilled prophecies. I am no longer held in the grip of sin and death because of Jesus' resurrection from the dead. What Jesus did by His cross and resurrection gives me the benefit of eternal life. If I die, I will not stay dead. I'll be lying there in the grave, and suddenly I will hear His voice and will be raised up from the dead because of my faith, thus defeating the power of death, which are the wages of sin that power ruled over me.

> Marvel not at this: for the hour is coming when all that are in the graves shall hear his voice, and they shall come forth; they that have done good, unto the resurrection of life; and they that have done evil, unto the resurrection of damnation. (John 5:28–29)

> The wicked is driven away in his wickedness: but the righteous hath hope in his death. (Proverbs 14:32)

You were created to have eternal fellowship with God, but sin deceives you into thinking otherwise. Sin deceives us. Sin destroys relationships; sin numbs us and makes us apathetic, just like crack cocaine addicts who don't care about anything or anyone except getting the drug to get high. That drug infects them just like sin infects us. Sin contaminates us and isolates us from God. Jesus came to heal our relationships with God and with each other. The way in which Jesus dealt with our sin issue once and for all is called the cross. His blood was the atonement that we all needed because it released us from the power of sin and restored us in relationship to God.

> But if we walk in the light, as he is in the light, we have fellowship one with another, and the blood of Jesus Christ his Son cleanseth us from all sin. (1 John 1:7)

If we could say that all the laws in the Bible can be identified as a violation of some type of relationship, then we could safely say that God is very interested our relationship with Him and with others. The basis of sin is relational violation. He is interested in what we say, do, and think with others and with Him. Salvation is not all about you being saved from hell. Salvation is about your relationship with God. What are we saved from? We are saved from death, which is isolation from God, and we are saved by faith to have relationship with the living God. So we are saved from hell for relationship. Remember Matthew 7:23? Jesus said,

> Not everyone who saith to me Lord, Lord, shall enter the kingdom of heaven; but he that doeth the will of my Father which is in heaven. Many will say to me in that day, Lord, Lord, have we not prophesied in thy name and in thy name cast out devils? And in thy name done many wonderful works? And then will I profess unto them, I never knew you: depart from me, ye that work iniquity.

Knowing God, being in a relationship, and having intimacy is what God desires with us. Going through empty, legalistic motions or even performing miracles without relationship means that many people will hear on that day God speak those awful words, "Depart from Me ye that work iniquity."

God provides the starting place for our relationship, which is the cross of Jesus Christ. He provides the sacrifice for sin, the forgiveness, the grace, and many other things we need for our restoration. We provide the faith, and the result is relationship. Reading the Word, having faith, the cross, and all of our Christian experience, including prophecy, lead us into a loving relationship with God.

Losing and Finding

Matthew 10:39 says, "He that finds his life shall lose it: and he that loseth his life for my sake shall find it." I understand about the losing my life part. For years I have heard pastors speak on the "losing my life" part of that verse. I know that verse shows me it is not all about me, my plans, my desires, my goals, my hobbies, or my thing. The "losing my life" part includes the process of letting go of my right to be angry or my desire to be self-justified, my agenda, my secret thought life, my malice, my pet peeves, my greed, and so on. I know that when I come to God humbly, it is all about His plan for my life. When I submit all that I am and all that I have to Him and His purposes, it is called losing my life, and that is what Colossians 3:3 calls a life hidden in Christ. What do I find when I come to God in that humility?

I will tell you a wonderful open secret. It is so obvious in the Scriptures, and it never loses its power to amaze. When I do all those things to lose my life for Christ, it is then that I find that God is all about me. Everything He does and every word He speaks is for my eternal benefit. He created this whole universe as a testimony for us so that we will know Him. I can look up at the evening sky at the heavens and in a small way understand the vastness of His glory. Anytime I call on His name, He listens. He listens to every prayer. Not even one thing escapes His attention. The Lord is never somewhere else, He is never too busy, and He is always lovingly fixated on us. Psalm 139:17–18 says, "How precious also are thy thoughts unto me, O God! How great is the sum of them! If I should count them, they are more in number than the sand: when I awake, I am still with thee." God's thoughts of you are more in number than the grains of sand. Have you ever tried to count the number of grains of sand in even one handful of sand? How great is the sum of them—wow! God never sleeps; He never slumbers (Ps. 121:4). He adores us even though we often stumble and fail.

Isaiah 49:16 says, "Behold I have graven thee upon the palms of my hands ..." The image I want you to see here is that the Lord did not just write you on the palms of His hands with a pen. No! The image here is one of cutting or chiseling with a sharp knife. God has put your name onto the palms of His hands with permanency. I believe that the verse out of Isaiah may have been an allusion to the crucifixion. In ancient times, the wrist was looked at as a part of the hand. The wrist would've been the part of Jesus' hand that the nails were driven through. Maybe we could say that Jesus has graven you upon His hands with the nails that were driven through His hands and into His cross. That is the image of the everlasting relationship with you that He desires. I believe that when we see Jesus we will see Him with the wounds He received from the crucifixion. Zechariah 13:6 says, "And one shall say unto him, what are these wounds in thine hands? Then he shall answer, those with which I was wounded in the house of my friends."

No one on this planet can be as close to you as the Lord. Whenever I call on Him, from wherever I am, no matter how I am feeling, for whatever reason, no matter who I am, He hears me. He never asks me why I am calling out to Him; He just listens to me and hears every word I speak. Just as a parent bends over to hear the words that his or her little child speaks, so God inclines His ear to us. Psalm 17:6 says, "I have called upon thee, for thou wilt hear me, O God: incline thine ear unto me and hear my speech." Psalm 116:2 says, "Because he hath inclined his ear unto me, therefore will I call upon him as long as I live." Name one person alive who can hear and remember every word you have said, know everything you have thought, see everything you've done, and love you so completely. You can't have total twenty-four/seven access to a person, but you have that kind of free access to God. "O taste and see that the Lord is good: blessed is the man that trusteth in him" (Ps. 34:8).

Saving Something Precious

Have you ever saved the drawings your little child has done? You put those precious little drawings up on the refrigerator with magnets. Of course, many of you have done that. You hang those drawings up for all to see. You exhibit your child's drawings because you are proud of what your child has done. You show your little ones how much you love them by saving and displaying their artwork.

I saved my kids' drawings for many years. They knew I was saving their drawings, and they would come to me with a picture they had drawn and ask me, "Daddy, do you want to save it?" I saved their drawings for years because they were like a treasure to me. Sometimes when I looked through all those pages of drawings, I would remember when they were small. I looked forward to the time when I would put them all in a scrapbook and give it to them. Before each of my children turned thirty, I went to one of those scrapbook places bought a scrapbook and some materials and made a special scrapbook of all their drawings and photos and gave it to them on their thirtieth birthdays.

God loves us in that same way. He lovingly adores us and is proud of us. He is like the parent who saves his or her child's drawings and displays them. It may sound strange, but do you know that God saves every one of your prayers? It is true—He saves your prayers. They are a treasure to Him that He keeps forever. Just like your parents who saved your drawings, each time you pray to God, God saves that prayer. Listen to what it says in Revelation 5:8. "And when he had taken the book, the four beasts and four and twenty elders fell down before the Lamb, having every one of them harps, and golden vials [most versions say 'bowls'] full of odors, which are the prayers of the saints." The odors are your prayers. Your prayers are in those golden bowls and have been saved by God. He saves your prayers not in bowls made of something common like wood, but He saves your prayers in special bowls made of gold. Those prayers are a sweet smell to God. You and your prayers are so precious to the Lord.

It Is All about Relationship

Do you see what God is all about? Everything He does, He does for our benefit. The cross of Christ is all about forgiveness. Do you know what forgiveness is? Please understand that forgiveness is relationship restoration. When we see the cross of Christ, we are looking at what God did to restore relationship with everyone on this earth. Losing your life for His sake is where you begin to see this; it is how you find your life in Christ. His intent is to build loving, joyful, intimate relationships with you and me. That is the loving nature of our God. He builds up relationships with us by prophecy, the law, the prophets, and His Word and through Bible stories that are our examples for living, by chastening, by His grace. He builds relationship by His eagerness to forgive, by the cross and the blood sacrifice of Jesus, by the power of the resurrection, by the indwelling of the Holy Spirit, and by His great love. In so many ways, He shows His love for us.

Way back when God was creating the worlds, He said in Genesis 1:26–27:

> And God said, Let us make man in our image, after our likeness; and let them have dominion over the fish of the sea, and over the fowl of the air, and over the cattle, and over all the earth, and over every creeping thing that creepeth upon the earth. And God created man in his own image, in the image of God created he him; male and female created he them.

I believe that these verses show the trinity in the plurality of the words *us* and *our* that God uses when He talks about making mankind. But there is another very significant meaning in the way He created man that shows His love for us. He created man in His own image. God created us to look like Him. He didn't create us to look different than He does; He wanted us to look the same. There is a certain closeness in being the same that being different does not permit. He wants us to be close not only because of the love He has for us, but He even wants us to look Him. It is like being related. Now that is close!

You have read 1 John 1:7, which says, "If we walk in the light, as He is in the light, we have fellowship one with another and the blood of Jesus Christ cleanses us from all sin." The word *fellowship* in that verse is the Greek word *Koinonia*. That word means "partnership, participation, communication, communion, social intercourse, participation." [Strong's Exhaustive Concordance of the Bible by World Publishers Inc.] It is a deep closeness and interactive relationship with God. So God uses our obedience to walk in the light to build Koinonia with us, active, intimate closeness. Once trust is established, maybe by seeing fulfilled prophecy, then we move on into the closeness of Koinonia. That is what God ultimately desires of us—Koinonia.

God gave us His Word. We call it the Bible. He used men as His pen to write His words to us. The Bible is His Word to help us understand who He is and what He expects from us. It shows us the result of our faith, our wonderful inheritance. The whole Bible helps us to know what He is like and how to have a relationship with Him. The cross of Christ is the point that God takes care of our sin issue and removes that roadblock to relationship. The whole world can now come through faith and into relationship based on what Jesus did on the cross to remove the consequences for our transgressions and give us an entrance into His divine nature.

Jesus completed the requirements of the law, and He was proven by prophecy to be the Messiah and our God. These are two powerful proofs that say He alone was worthy to be the Lamb of God to redeem man while nailed to the cross. That single act of sacrifice makes us able to have relationship with the Father through the Son with the help of the Holy Spirit. From creation to the words of God to the cross to prophecy, God is reaching out to all of us to be in a close relationship, and that, my friends, is what He is all about. His use of prophecy is to bring us to His loving nature and to be close forever.

In Luke 6:40, Jesus says, "The servant is not above his master: but every one that is perfect shall be as his master." We as servants seek to be like Jesus. Jesus calls the servant that is like his master "perfect," meaning complete or restored. We want to learn about Him, and we want to know Him; we want to be close to Him. We want to have God's heart for people because when we see God's loving and tender heart for people, it changes us. It creates the same loving heart in us for people that the Lord has. When we see God's loving heart for people, it changes us and helps us to leave our conditional love and legalisms behind and move on in unconditional love.

Of course legalism is living by rules, but living by unconditional love is living by the Spirit. Christians who have undergone a change of heart by the Spirit of God and by experiencing God's great love draw others to faith in the Lord. If God's desire is that none should perish, as John 3:16 says, then it is no wonder that the people who love God should also love others unconditionally to bring them into the kingdom. God is all inclusive with the call of "whosoever believeth in him" (John 3:16). Whosoever will believe in Jesus can come and partake of the relationship that is awaiting them in God.

Chapter 13

God's Glory, Our Benefit

Matthew 5:13–16 says:

> Ye are the salt of the earth; but if the salt has lost his savour, wherewith shall it be salted? It is thenceforth good for nothing, but to be cast out, and to be trodden under foot of men. Ye are the light of the world. A city that is set on a hill cannot be hid. Neither do men light a candle, and put it under a bushel, but on a candle stick; and it giveth light unto all that are in the house. Let your light so shine before men, that they may see your good works, and glorify your Father which is in heaven.

Jesus told His disciples this passage immediately after talking about the Beatitudes. We are part of the reason God is glorified. We can glorify God in the way that we do things. In the above passage, we can glorify God when others see our good works. We may have personal ministry to the homeless or volunteer in a hospital or many other ways that we serve in the kingdom of God. That work we do in service to God glorifies God when we work not according to our own desires or for our own benefit but out of our appreciation for what the Lord has done for us.

Now we can glorify God by the things we do, and there are things God does to glorify Himself. As mentioned before, He brought the Jews into Egypt and delivered them out of their bondage. God used Egypt as a harsh surrogate to birth a nation that would be used to glorify Him. The Jews glorified God in their deliverance from Egypt, and God glorified Himself. Sure, the Jews obeyed God in their deliverance from Egypt—they were obedient to go—but really they were more than willing to go out after four hundred years of slavery and onto freedom.

The Promised Land was a narrow piece of land that bridged two continents; it was God's prime business location for Israel. The workers at this prime business location were the Jews. They were to show everyone who passed through their land how loving and gracious the Lord God is for the purpose of bringing other nations to serve the Lord. At times through history God has glorified Himself, and we can glorify Him too. It is all for the same purpose—that of bringing many others into the kingdom of God. We glorify God by the things we do in service to Him, but there are very special times when God's glory is revealed in something that He does. Our service to Him glorifies God, but the works He does to glorify Himself are for our benefit.

God's glory is seen or declared by at least the fifteen things that follow.

1. By things God has made (Ps. 19:1, 72:19)

2. By things God has done (Ex. 15:1–11)

3. By things we do (Matt. 5:16)

4. By the nation of Israel (Jeremiah. 30:19)

5. By the Gentiles (Isaiah. 62:2, Rom. 15:9)

6. By Jesus for the Father (John 17:4)

7. By the Father for Jesus (John 17:5)

8. By His presence in the temple (Isaiah. 60:7)

9. By our worship (Ps. 96:7–9, Rev. 15:4)

10. By His holy name (Ps. 29:2)

11. By our praises (Ps. 50:23, 86:12)

12. By our declaration (Ps. 96:3)

13. By His Word (Ps. 56:4, Acts 13:48)

14. By His name (Isaiah. 57:15, Matt. 6:9, John 12:28, Acts 3:16, 19:17, Phil. 2:9–11)

15. By prophetic fulfillment (Ex. 12:40–42, Matt. 1:22–23, Luke 2:25–32)

Does God have an obsessive need to have us glorify Him? No, but He is completely deserving of glory because of who He is. However, there is a purpose for God to be glorified, and it is the same purpose as the purpose for all prophecy: it is for creating and deepening relationships. Certainly God has glory because He is God; He is far above us in glory. But understand that it is *our* extreme need to see God glorified. God knows it is for *our* benefit to see Him glorified. When we see God do something—a miracle or a prophetic fulfillment—then He is glorified, and we are humbled and know that He is God. Then we come to Him in faith and trust. If you were standing on the shore of the Red Sea and saw the waters part and your whole nation passed through the waters on dry ground while Pharaoh's army was drowned, you would've seen God glorify Himself. He saved you and your people from death, and you would be drawn to the one who had done all this.

Faith on a Mountain

Let's say that you are one of the children of Israel in the time of Elijah the prophet, about twenty-nine hundred years ago. Every king of Israel since the split with Judah have been evil worshipers of false gods and it is even more so now under the rule of King Ahab. It is a time of widespread worship of Baal and Asherah (Asherah was another false god). From King Ahab and his wife Queen Jezebel to the least, just about everyone worships Baal. Your family has worshipped Baal for a long time here in the Northern Kingdom of Israel.

One of your relatives tells you that King Ahab has sent for all the people of Israel to go to Mt Carmel. The 450 prophets of Baal and the 400 prophets of Asherah will be there with the prophet Elijah on Mt. Carmel. There are 950 prophets all gathered together in one place against Elijah. It will be a test of fire to see whose God is God (1 Kings 18:17–40). If Baal answers by fire, then he is God, but if the Lord answers by fire, then He is God.

You are skeptical, thinking that Baal just might be the one that answers by fire. You want to see Elijah embarrassed. You think he is the one who brought the drought to Israel that has ravaged your family's crops. You eagerly leave with your friends and family and go to Mt. Carmel to see just who will answer by fire. Your group joins many others on their way to see this sight. Many people from all over Israel want to see this spectacle. Mt. Carmel is not far from your family's home, and your journey is not a long one. You arrive at the base of the mountain and start to climb. As you climb higher on the mountain, you can see many thousands of people coming from all over Israel. At the top of the mountain, you find Elijah with the prophets of Baal. You arrive as a group a couple of hours before noon. Elijah's voice seems to carry down the mountain to all the people's ears. Elijah asks everyone sitting on the mountain how long they will waver between two opinions. He says if the Lord be God, then follow Him, but if Baal, then follow him. No one dares to answer him because they all fear this prophet of God.

You watch as the prophets of Baal prophesy and worship after their manner of service to Baal. There is a slaughtered bull on a beautiful altar of Baal. The prophets of Asherah eat at Queen Jezebel's table every day. Their garments are beautifully adorned. These prophets of Baal are all so serious calling out to Baal to answer by fire from heaven and consume the bull that is upon their altar. Certainly Baal will hear and answer their call by fire. You expect Baal to answer their call at any second.

At midday, Elijah starts to mock them, saying that Baal is daydreaming, away in another country, or sleeping. The prophets of Baal become desperate and start ritualistically cutting themselves with knives, crying out louder, and leaping upon the altar where they have laid the bull in sacrifice to Baal. They are falsely prophesying all sorts of strange things. They look tired and like they have been at this for a long time.

You take out the food you have brought and eat a meal while watching this wild scene. It is getting late in the day, and there has been no answer from Baal. The prophets of Baal are starting to look very foolish. The sun is sinking lower in the sky, and it is coming close to the time of the evening sacrifice. There has been no time in history that someone has challenged Baal like this. At first you thought, *How dare anyone challenge our god like this*, but now you are not so sure. You think, *Maybe Baal just wants to test our faith by delaying his answer by fire.* This is a showdown, and you become interested more and more to see who will prove themselves—Baal or the Lord. You start to doubt that Baal is going to answer and think that maybe Elijah's God will answer by fire.

The time for Baal to answer by fire has ended and now it is Elijah's turn. Elijah stands up and calls for the people to come near. You move closer to Elijah. Everyone's eyes are upon Elijah as he takes twelve stones, and with them he repairs the broken-down altar of the Lord and digs a trench around the altar. He does the work himself. He looks like he has just plain clothes on and no fine attire like the prophets of Baal. He takes wood and arranges it on the altar. he cuts a bull in pieces and lays the pieces upon the altar. He takes a shovel and digs a trench all the way around the altar. He is working slowly and steadily.

The prophets of Baal and Ashera stand nearby exhausted murmuring amongst themselves and watching the prophet of God.

Elijah commands that four barrels be filled with water and to pour it on the sacrifice and on the wood. The people obey his word and do it. Elijah commands that they do it a second and a third time. The water is all over the place. The sacrifice is soaked, the wood is all wet, and the trench is filled up with water too. You think there is no way and that even if the Lord God answers by fire, the sacrifice is just too wet; it will just smoke and not catch fire. Why is Elijah soaking everything? Is he trying to make it harder on his own God to answer by fire? It doesn't make any sense.

Everyone is looking at the sky and at Elijah. Will the Lord answer? Elijah speaks so everyone can hear him: "Hear me, O Lord, hear me, that this people may know that thou art the Lord God, and that thou hast turned their heart back again." Without any pause, the fire falls down out of heaven, and it is huge and hot. Everyone, including the priests of Baal and the king, runs back away from the heat of the fire. It completely consumes the sacrifice and the wood, and the flames turn the water in the trench to a huge column of steam from the top of the mountain.

You are astonished and fall on your face, and now you know without a doubt that the Lord, He is God. Everyone with you and the whole crowd is doing the same thing, and all the people are saying over and over, "The Lord, He is God, the Lord, He is God." Now you know why Elijah doused the sacrifice the wood and the trench with so much water. He knew the answer from the real God would be a huge ball of fire that would consume everything on and around the altar. Now everything you knew and trusted in has dried up. The real God has shown everyone that He is the only true God. It was a miracle. It was proof positive, and now you have decided to have faith in the Lord God.

It is doubtful if Elijah was taking a chance to see if the Lord would answer by fire that day on Mt. Carmel. It could be that Elijah was fully assured that the Lord would answer in the way He did by the fire from the sky. If he was not so assured, then why would Elijah have doused the sacrifice, the wood, and the trench with water? The Bible doesn't record the Lord saying anything to Elijah to set up a sacrifice and that the Lord would answer by fire, but Elijah was a man of God and it is very possible that he knew what the Lord was going to do.

You can see from the story that the Lord proved who was God that day on Mt. Carmel in front of all the 950 false prophets and the people. God glorified Himself in front of all the people by answering Elijah's prayer with fire. The result was faith coming to the people who were watching. Now God absolutely deserves all glory, but He glorifies Himself for our benefit. When we see God glorified like what God did on Mt. Carmel, it starts faith in us. Elijah knew that God would glorify Himself in front of all the people of Israel. It is possible that God wanted Elijah to tell Ahab to bring all the people of Israel and all the false prophets there to Carmel to slay the false prophets. Certainly Elijah couldn't kill 950 false prophets all by himself. Once the Lord was glorified, the people followed Elijah's direction and rose up and killed all the false prophets. God was not only glorified that day and did not just start faith in all the people; He was taking out the false religious system too.

Our faith in God starts the flow of benefits that God promises to everyone who has faith. We receive every benefit God has promised to people who believe in Him—benefits like salvation, eternal life, being in heaven with Jesus, and many others. On Mt. Carmel, the people of Israel started to have faith after seeing God glorified. When people come to the Lord in faith after seeing God glorified, their assignment is to glorify God so others may also see their good works, and God is glorified again, which draws even more people to the faith.

Life is not all about us; we have seen that before. We lose our lives, crucify the flesh, and spend our lives as living sacrifices in service to our King. On one hand, we have everything we can obtain and do in this life. On the other hand is everything God has promised to those who live a life of obedient faith. Which is better? The things we receive for the life of faith are amazing and far better than anything we could possibly gain or do here on this planet. God loves us, and everything He does is designed to draw us into a place where we have intimacy. Prophecy is so designed by God to bring us into relationship, and seeing God glorified works the same way. When we see God glorified by a prophetic fulfillment or in some miracle, like Elijah at Mt. Carmel, we are drawn to Him in faith. I'm sure that by just looking up at the night sky full of stars, some have started to believe in God. God works in at least the fifteen ways on the earlier list to show that He is glorified for the purpose of bringing people to Himself. Fulfilled prophecy glorifies God because He is able to make His words come to fulfillment.

Simeon in Luke 2:25–32 glorified God upon seeing fulfillment of prophecy.

> And behold there was a man in Jerusalem, whose name was Simeon; and the same man was just and devout, waiting for the consolation of Israel; and the Holy Ghost was upon him. And it was revealed unto him by the Holy Ghost, that he should not see death, before he had seen the Lord's Christ. And he came by the Spirit into the temple; and when the parents brought in the child Jesus, to do for him after the custom of the law, Then took he him up in his arms, and blessed God and said, "Lord, now lettest thou thy servant depart in peace, according to thy word: For mine eyes have seen thy salvation, Which thou hast prepared before the face of all people; A light to the Gentiles, and the glory of Israel."

Simeon glorified God upon seeing prophetic fulfillment in Jesus. Without prophetic fulfillment, there would've been no testimony of

God, no glorifying of God, and no creation of faith and trust, leading to relationship. God uses many things, like letting us see His glory in prophetic fulfillment. He uses the prophetic to accomplish many things, but we see that the purpose is to create relationship. It is like the roots of a giant tree—all the roots feed the rest of the tree. There are many facets of the relationship building process that God places before us to build a strong trust and faith in Him.

Our Hope for God's Glory

Throughout the Bible, God has been glorified. God has been glorified in His creation and in the deliverance or Israel from Egypt. He is glorified when we do good works and when He moves in mighty ways while we stand and watch what He does. He is glorified in many ways, and it is good to glorify Him in any way we can. "Whether therefore ye eat, or drink, or whatsoever ye do, do all to the glory of God" (1 Corinthians. 10:31).

God's glory affects us, and it should. It is amazing to see Him move in ways that are far beyond anything we can do. Sometimes we pray for God to be glorified in some way. We pray for God to be glorified in our workplaces, our schools, and our homes. We want to see Him lifted up in glory. As wonderful as it is to see God glorified, is that it? Is that all that there is—to pray and ask that God be glorified? I think we have to ask the question, "What is God's purpose for His glory to be seen?"

First let me say that God deserves all the glory we can give to Him. He is God, and all glory belongs to Him. We know that everything He does is for creating and deepening relationships. I think relationship building may also encompass God's glory. What should our reaction be? Our reaction and our hope is to see God glorified so that many people will see it, be drawn into faith and trust, and start their own relationships with the Lord.

It is God's heart to be in fellowship with us, and everything He does for us is to meet that desire. His faithfulness is shown to us so we can trust what He says will come to pass; He will do what He says. His glory works the same way. Faithfulness is in His nature and glory is what He has and is deserving of, but both of these things about God draw us to Him. It is our desire and hope to see God glorified. It is from coming to know the heart of God for people that our own heart is changed to be like Him. Our hope and desire is to see many come to know Him by that glory. When we do that, God's heart for people is in us.

CHAPTER 14
The Covenant Relationship

Webster's Dictionary describes a covenant as a "formal, solemn; and binding agreement; contract; a written agreement or promise usually under seal between two or more parties, esp. for the performance of some action."[6] A contract is binding, meaning that force could be used upon one of the parties in the contract to perform a part of the contract, usually in some form of punishment and/or reward.

We know that the Lord has given covenants (contracts) to people based on the relationship between the Lord and a group of people. The contract between the Jews and the Lord was written out and called the law. The Ten Commandments were written on stone tablets and put in the ark of the covenant. You could call the ark of the covenant, which was a box with a lid, the box of the contract. The lid to the box was called the mercy seat. The Ten Commandments were chiseled onto two stone tablets and put into this box. Those two stone tablets represented the whole law, and that was the contract, thus the box was called the Ark of the Covenant. The whole law was not put onto stone tablets and put into the Ark of the Covenant because the law was huge and the box wasn't big enough to carry it all. A representation of the law was laid in the box, and that was enough to call it the Ark of the Covenant.

The covenant described the terms of the relationship between the Lord and the descendants of Abraham, called at times Hebrews, children of

Israel, or the Jews. We often look at the covenant as being only between the Jews and the Lord because we can see that contract written out in the first five books of our Bible, which were written by a man called the lawgiver—Moses. If it were true that God only dealt with the people with whom He had a covenant, then He would not deal with anyone else according to the terms of the contract. But we know that isn't true. God did indeed deal with many other people according to the covenant—people who were outside of the covenant with the Jews.

The story of Jonah was a case in point. Jonah was sent to the people of Nineveh, who were not Jews; they were Assyrians. He bore a message from God to the great city of Nineveh. That message said the Ninevites would be overthrown for their wickedness. It could be effectively argued that the Assyrians had no written covenant or agreement with God that was binding like the Jews had. So why was God going to punish the Assyrians for their wickedness when they had not violated any contract? Does God like to go around and arbitrarily punish people outside of the contract He had with the Jews? Of course God does not indiscriminately punish people without reason. Even though the people of Nineveh had no written covenant with God like the Jews had, God is still bound to the people of Nineveh and the rest of the world. God is still their Creator and their God, whether they had a written covenant or not.

In the beginnings of the Jewish nation, God put the Jews in a special land that bridged two continents. Why there? It was a small slice of land wedged between the two superpowers of the ancient world—Egypt and Mesopotamia. Egypt was always called Egypt, but the land of Mesopotamia had different names for the nations there, known at different times as Assyria, Babylon, and Persia. Remember the old question about what the three most important things are to have in order to start a successful business? The answer was, "Location, location, location." I think God knew this long before we did when He created the continents and chose the land between two continents and two ancient superpowers as the location for the people who would represent Him to the world.

The special relationship between God and the Jews had a purpose. That purpose was to love God and represent the Lord to the people of those two nations as they passed through Israel from one end to the other for commerce and travel. As people of those two superpowers passed through the land of Israel they learned about the God of the Jews and the special contract they had with their God. The Promised Land was a special location that was supposed to be a place where the Jews witnessed to the world.

Of course there were many times in Israel's history when Israel and later Judah didn't serve the Lord. They lived their lives in the opposite way from what God intended, and their witness to those nations was greatly diminished. But as the Assyrians and Egyptians passed through Israel, they did learn about the God of the Jews. They learned how God delivered the Jews from Egyptian slavery and about other examples of what God did in the midst of them. They learned about the covenant relationship and the law. Some of those travelers passing through Israel may've come to faith in God because of the Jews' witness.

We often think the people of Israel were the only people who served the Lord God, but there are many biblical examples of faith in the Lord outside of the nation of Israel. In Jonah's time, the people reacted to Jonah's prophecy with sackcloth and ashes. That was a Jewish way of mourning, but the Assyrians knew about it.

Where did the wise men come from? They bore gifts to the newborn Messiah (Matt. 2:1–12). They came from the east; east from Israel is Mesopotamia. The wise men knew of the prophecies concerning the Messiah, so they knew about the covenant. The wise men had faith in the God of Israel and were willing to make a long and perilous journey to bring Him precious gifts of gold, frankincense, and myrrh.

Remember the Ethiopian eunuch? He was a man of great authority in Ethiopia, and he was reading the prophecies of Isaiah in Acts 8:27–39. If he had great authority, then he would be known in Ethiopia as a man of faith in the God of the Jews.

Remember on the day of Pentecost at the baptism of the Holy Ghost in Acts 2:6. The disciples were speaking in new tongues (languages), and all the people who were present heard the disciples speak in their own languages when the disciples were speaking in different languages that the disciples had never studied or spoken before. We know that there were many people in Jerusalem celebrating Pentecost from different nations because they spoke different languages and they understood the disciples' new tongues. There were many people with faith in the God of the Jews outside of Israel.

When Jonah came through the city of Nineveh, the people of that city would've already known about the God of the Jews. Jonah didn't have to explain where he was from or who he was; his clothing showed he was a Jew. The people of Nineveh would have seen Jonah and known he was a Jew and a follower of the Most High God. When he came to the city in about 800 BC, the story of the Jews' deliverance from Egypt had been around for seven hundred years. Next to the story of the Noah and the flood, the biggest story of that time was the Jews' deliverance from Egypt. It is a safe bet to say that the entire world knew about the God of the Jews and about major events from Israel's history.

The Assyrians, Babylonians, and Persians have had their own history with the Lord of Israel. Remember that Israel spent seventy years in Babylon according to the prophecy of Jeremiah (Jer. 25:11–12). In the time of King Nebuchadnezzar of Babylon, Daniel, a Jew, was promoted to second in command of the world's most-powerful nation. Nebuchadnezzar had a dream that made him fear greatly, but he couldn't remember it. He wanted the wise men of Babylon to tell him what the dream was and its meaning. The wise men of Babylon didn't know what it was or the meaning, so the king ordered all the wise men to be killed. Daniel was gifted by God to interpret dreams, and he declared the dream and its meaning to the king. The story of what God did in that land of Babylon was published throughout the known world at that time.

At a later time, when Nebuchadnezzar was restored to his throne after living like a beast of the field for a while, the king made a proclamation of faith in the Lord God of Israel in Daniel 4:29–37. There might have been many in Babylon who decided, like the king, to follow the God of these Jews who were living among the Babylonians. Certainly the Jews living in Babylon interacted with the people living there. There may have been Babylonians who passed their faith from generation to generation from Jonah's time to Daniel's time about 250 years later. Babylonians in Daniel's time might not have been surprised that a Jew would know and interpret king Nebuchadnezzar's dream because of the story of Jonah and about Joseph in Egypt. Babylonians and Assyrians understood that the God of the Jews knew secrets and revealed the future.

The Jews were like God's own visual aid to the world, showing what relationship with God looked like. They were supposed to be God's representatives of what the blessedness of relationship with God looked like. It could be that this was the ultimate view that the Lord intended the world to see in the Jews. The Lord wanted to show the whole world how much the Jews enjoyed being loved and blessed by God. The purpose of this view, of course, was to draw as many people into the covenant relationship as possible. The covenant was written out for the Jews for the purpose of representing the Lord to the other nations to draw everyone close to the Lord.

Remember John 3:16? "For God so loved the world, that he gave his only begotten Son, that whosoever believeth in him should not perish, but have everlasting life." "God so loved the world" is a statement that is not just tied to the Jews and the law. Maybe we could say that before

Jesus came the Lord so loved the world so that whosoever would come into covenant relationship would not perish but have everlasting life. God is unchangeable, and so is His love for us.

> And he took the cup, and gave thanks, and said, Take this and divide it among yourselves: For I say unto you, I will not drink of the fruit of the vine, until the kingdom of God shall come. And he took the bread and gave thanks, and brake it, and gave unto them, saying, This is my body which is given for you: this do in remembrance of me. Likewise also the cup after supper, saying, This cup is the new testament in my blood, which is shed for you. (Luke 22:17–20)

We know from John 3:16 that God is very willing for everyone to come to faith in Him. The New Testament is written in Jesus' own blood, and was shed for the whole world, which includes every Gentile who had no written covenant with God.

We are in a relationship with God because He has not only made us but also sustains us. Our next breath, our next heartbeat is given to us from God, and at the appointed time, both will stop and we will go to Him for judgment. Sometimes we think that not having faith will help us escape the judgment of God, but that is just wrong thinking. God wants so much for us to have faith and relationship with Him in this life so that we can be with Him for eternity. We are His, and He wants to see His children doing well, as all parents want for their children. Doing well with God is being close to Him in a relationship that has great depth and breadth.

God will judge the whole world, Jew and Gentile alike, according to His righteousness for what we've done in this life. Our relationship with God is inescapable; we are intricately bound to Him because He made us. God's purpose was to create relationship with the people who had no covenant through the people who had the covenant. The purpose of Jesus' death on the cross and His resurrection was the same: to create relationship with everyone. Technically all people of the earth are in a contractual relationship with God and every person—covenant and non-covenant people—will stand before the judgment seat of Christ. However, God's real desire is to be close to us and for us to enjoy His extraordinary greatness.

Of course there are many more biblical examples of faith outside of Israel. It may be said that because of these major stories, there was faith in the Lord all over the world through history. The point of all this is that God is tied to us in relationship. That relationship is obtained by everyone who is alive now and everyone who has ever lived, with or without faith. We are all responsible to God for what we have done and the decisions we have made about believing in Him.

What should our relationship to the Lord look like today? I'm not so sure there is only one example of what a person who follows the Lord would look like, but there are some definite things that must be in a believer's life. Believers must have a Bible-based faith in the Lord. They are humble about their own lives and not self-promoting. They are obedient to the Lord and have a willingness to serve in whatever capacity the Lord wants. They have joy and peace, and the Holy Spirit leads them in their decisions and actions. They pray continually through the day and read the Word to know the Lord through what is written in the Bible. Having said all that, I'm sure there are many believers who don't look like every detail I've listed who are just fine and their relationship with the Lord is okay.

What is it like to be in a relationship with God? We know how to be in relationship with people we can see and feel and talk with, but how do we "do" relationship with God, whom we can't see or carry on an interactive conversation with? We don't have to have faith that the people around us exist because we can see them. Most of us have trouble in our relationships at some point with people we can see. We ignore what someone is saying, so we can catch something someone is saying on TV and it offends them, and we are in a place where we have to apologize and ask their forgiveness.

Do we ignore God in the same fashion? Sure we do. We seem to have flaws in our ability to partake in our relationships properly. It is in our sin nature. We are all in sloppy agape relationships. We try to love each other, but it is messy, with offense, repentance, and forgiveness. Sometimes there is unforgiveness, also called holding a grudge, which we have to work on so we can truly forgive everyone. Many believers are in a long process of forgiveness for those who have been deeply offended. We try to work out our relationship with the Lord in the best way that we can, but that often looks the same as people without faith.

Remember that Proverbs 3:5–6 says, "Trust in the Lord with all thine heart; and lean not unto thine own understanding. In all thy ways acknowledge him and he shall direct thy paths." This verse is quite well known, but it is about an interactive relationship with God. We do the trust part and the leaning not on our own understanding part, acknowledging Him in all our ways, and then something wonderful happens. God directs our paths. He directs our lives and our relationships. He actively engages us and has our best interests at heart. Our prayers are the time when we can have that interactive time with the Lord. We get so caught up in the asking part of prayer that we don't take time for the listening part of prayer. We often fail to get what we need from the Lord because we are too busy. Take the time to listen to God in your prayers. Ask the Lord if there is anything He would like to say to you. Lord, I will listen for Your voice in my prayers. I will look for Your direction in my life.

CHAPTER 15

Prophetic Prayers

There are many good books about prayer that cover many aspects of our communication with God. Maybe you have read a good book on prayer recently. Prayer is communicating with our Father through the Son with the aid of the Holy Spirit. It is for praise and worship, it is for making petitions, and it is used as a time to listen for God's voice. We pray for our needs corporately as a church, individually, and for others.

Prayer has a prophetic side to it too. We pray and make our requests and have faith that if we ask according to His will, God will answer us and grant our prayers. We pray for God to be glorified at our schools or workplaces and in our witness for Him. We pray for someone to be saved and for God to bring many witnesses to someone for the purpose of pointing him or her to Jesus. We are asking God to forgive, to heal, to save, to empower ministry, to comfort, and to help us be more and more like Jesus. Prayer is always for future things to happen, never for the past to be changed.

The Holy Spirit helps us with our prayers to the Father. Romans 8:26–27 says:

> Likewise the Spirit also helpeth our infirmities [weakness]; for we know not what to pray for as we ought: but the Spirit itself maketh intercession for us with groanings which cannot be uttered. And he that searcheth the hearts knoweth what

is the mind of the Spirit, because he maketh intercession for
the saints according to the will of God.

The Holy Spirit makes intercession on our behalf in our prayers because
we sometimes don't know what to pray for. Whether a situation is
complicated or the will of God is hard to determine given the circumstance,
and we just don't know what to do or how to pray. In these situations, the
Spirit steps in to help us pray the will of God. This is true partnering
with God in the prophetic because the will of God is yet to happen,
and what the Spirit is helping us to pray for is God's will to become a
reality. An answer to prayer may be received later, after we have prayed
the prayer, so we are praying for future events to happen. It is in this
sense that we are joining with God to see the future happen through
His will and our prayers. We are partners in the future with God to
bring more people into the kingdom and into relationship with God.

Job number one for a basketball player is to shoot the basketball and
score points. If a basketball player can't shoot the ball, then he has to pass
the ball or start dribbling the ball. Our number-one job as Christians is
relationship with the Almighty, both nurturing our own relationship with
Him and bringing as many people as possible into that all-encompassing
love of Jesus Christ. Everything else is just a peripheral, like passing
the ball or dribbling.

Ultimately the goal of almost all prayers is to have a deepening relationship
with Jesus. Sure, we pray for the sick, we pray to have enough money to
pay the rent or buy food, but those are temporal needs. God answers
those prayers and meets many of those needs all the time. I think God
uses healing as an answer to prayer to give us reasons for our faith,
and that is relational. Imagine that the reason for God answering a
prayer for the sick is relationship building. Of course, the first thing
we do when we receive an answer to prayer and someone is healed of
a sickness, injury, or disease is to glorify Him and know that God has

answered our prayers. That, my friend, is relationship building. Miracles are wonderful relationship builders from God.

We never pray for something to happen in the past. We don't pray a prayer that says, "Lord, please forgive my dead friend." We don't pray that kind of prayer because our dead friend's life has been lived. It is over, and whatever he or she did in this life is now sealed and will be judged. It can't be changed by our prayers. We pray for future things, and in this sense we pray things into existence, similar to the prophetic. Maybe we have a vision for someone to be saved or a vision for a Christian orphanage to be built in a distant land for the purpose of raising children up in the Lord. Maybe we pray for a missionary's work to prosper or for our neighborhood or city to have a revival. We participate with God for future things for the sake of the kingdom. In a way, an answer to prayer is similar to prophetic fulfillment because we see the results of what we have prayed for come to be answered. Answers to prayers are like prophetic fulfillments, but with prayer, we have partnered with God in the answers to prayer.

Did you know that there are prayers in the Bible that contain elements of the prophetic? Quite a few prayers have at least a portion of the prayer that contains prophecy, or at least a reference to prophecy. Prophetic prayers are for an event that has not happened yet and for something to happen in the future. Prayers are prophetic; Jesus told us to pray for things in the future too. One very well-known prayer that He taught us to pray is what we call the Lord's Prayer, and it has a prophetic part. Jesus taught us to pray in Matthew 6:9–13 and in Luke 11:2–4. In Matthew 6:10 a verse from that prayer says, "Thy kingdom come. Thy will be done on earth as it is in heaven." God's kingdom isn't here on the earth yet, but we know that one day it will be. The words "thy kingdom come" have a broad application, from the second coming of Jesus to the millennial rule of Jesus on earth and beyond. God's kingdom is coming in a very real way to this earth. This part of the Lord's Prayer directs us to pray for God's kingdom to be set up on earth, which is a future event when God's kingdom will come.

Jesus again told us to pray for the world's salvation. Matthew 9:37–38 says, "Then saith he unto his disciples, the harvest truly is plenteous, but the laborers are few: Pray ye therefore the Lord of the harvest, that he will send forth labourers into his harvest." This prayer has a prophetic flavor to it for the harvesting of souls. This is especially pertinent with the planet now home to seven billion people and projected to grow to nine billion by 2040. That's quite a large harvest.

In Matthew, Jesus is giving prophetic direction to a certain group of people and directs them to pray for the timing of a certain event. Matthew 24:15–21 says:

> When ye therefore shall see the abomination of desolation, spoken of by Daniel the prophet, stand in the holy place, (whoso readeth let him understand) Then let them which be in Judea flee into the mountains: Let him which is on the housetop not come down to take any thing out of his house: Neither let him which is in the field return back to take his clothes. And woe unto them that are with child and to them that give suck in those days! But pray ye that your flight be not in the winter, neither on the Sabbath day: For then shall be great tribulation, such as was not since the beginning of the world to this time no nor ever shall be.

Jesus is directing a specific group of people to pray about the timing of this abomination of desolation. Jesus is talking to Jews living in Judea, quite possibly at the time of the Antichrist, directing them to be ready and to be watching, but it also directs them to pray for the timing of this event to be advantageous to their flight.

We know these are Jews that Jesus directs His prophecy to because they are living in Judea and because of the mention of the Sabbath. He directs them to pray that this abomination not happen on the Sabbath because of the Sabbath laws, which restrict how far a Jew can travel on the Sabbath. The Sabbath day's journey mentioned in Joshua 3:4 as two thousand cubits (a cubit was the length from one's fingertip to the elbow, about eighteen inches) or about one thousand yards. This distance was interpreted differently at times in the Bible, but the furthest a Sabbath day's journey was interpreted to be was just over a mile before the short journey became work, which was forbidden in the law. A person walking that far had to stop to obey the law. Obviously people in that time will have a much further distance to go than a mile to flee this abomination.

This direction of this verse to flee is a sort of a "when you see that, do this" kind of a verse. If I was living in that time and had read Jesus' words on this and knew the time to flee was so short, then I would be in Boy Scout mode. I'd be prepared to go long in advance. In these verses in Matthew, we see Jesus directing a group of Jews in a very specific time and place to pray about the timing of the abomination. If you believe otherwise about the application of these verses, then please see that God is lovingly taking care of the people He is directing to pray. He takes care of His people and directs that care, even into the future.

We have another prayer with prophetic implications in Luke 21:36. "Watch ye therefore, and pray always, that ye may be accounted worthy to escape all these things that shall come to pass, and to stand before the Son of man." Jesus is talking prior to verse 36 about a time that may be similar to the above verses from Matthew 24. Jesus says, "Pray always that you be accounted worthy to escape all these things."

What things do we need to escape? Maybe the things we need to escape are a part of the tribulation in the end times. I think we can understand from that verse that there will be an accounting that will be decided in heaven at that time to see who is worthy to escape all the things that shall come to pass. We are directed to pray always that we will be accounted worthy to be included in the group that escapes all those things. The prophetic element in this prayer is the part that says, "All these things that shall come to pass." Because we are directed by the Lord to pray this way, this prayer should be an active and common prayer in the life of all believers. We hear the Lord's Prayer prayed all the time, but when have you heard someone pray that they be accounted worthy to escape the things that shall come to pass? It could be that the word *escape* from that verse is referring to the rapture, so maybe we are being directed to pray that we are worthy to go to heaven to meet Jesus in the rapture to escape the horrors of "these things."

Many of you have read Solomon's prayer in 1 Kings 8:22–53 and read it as a temple dedication prayer, but there is a prophetic element to it. In verse 24, Solomon references the prophetic promises God gave to David his father and fulfilled. "Thou spakest also with thy mouth, and hast fulfilled it with thine hand, as it is this day." Solomon saw God's faithfulness in the fulfillment of prophecy and acknowledged it in his prayer at the dedication of the temple. Solomon acknowledged that God is faithful by doing with His hand all the words that He speaks with His mouth.

We see that God directs people in very specific times to pray for things that possibly we haven't seen yet on the world stage. I admit that I pray the prayer for the Jews to have the proper season and day of the week to flee when they see the abomination in the temple.

Do you remember when Jesus cleansed the temple, driving out those who were selling things in the temple in Luke 19:44–46? Jesus said something that referenced Isaiah. Jesus quoted a part of Isaiah 56:7, which says in full, "Even them will I bring to my holy mountain, and make them joyful in my house of prayer: their burnt offerings and their sacrifices shall be accepted upon my altar; for mine house shall be called an house of prayer for all people." The "all people" part of that verse includes Gentiles. This verse has a twofold application. It applied in the time of Jesus to anyone who wanted to worship at the temple site. It is also a very prophetic verse with millennium-time application that is coming for both Jews and Gentiles, who will be worshipping together in the new temple praising Jesus. God's house, the temple, was not known as a house or prayer for all nations in Jesus' time, but the temple that will be built there might be known by that name.

I believe that every believer partakes of the prophetic with God when they pray because we pray for things to happen in the future with kingdom ramifications. Our prayers are a part of spiritual warfare when we pray the will of God into the future and against our common enemy. "For we wrestle not against flesh and blood, but against principalities, against the rulers of darkness of this world, against spiritual wickedness in High places" (Eph. 6:12). Is there spiritual wickedness and rulers of darkness now? Yes! We need to be in prayer not only about those things that concern our day-to-day lives and those of others but also offer up prayers for the future of our relatives, friends, and coworkers, our leaders, the Jews and Israel, and the world. If we know what is coming, then we can pray for the benefit of God's will to be done in the hearts of people who are seeking Him. God hears us when we pray and grants our request according to His will, and then He works in ways we cannot see to answer our petitions. This is the same way prophecy is fulfilled. I think the kingdom of God is very busy answering and working on prayer requests.

First Thessalonians 5:17 is a very short verse that says, "Pray without ceasing." I wonder about that verse in the light of what we know about the prophetic side to prayer. Are we being directed to partner with God in the prophetic continually, knowing that our citizenship is not of this world? I think so. Be a spiritual warrior in the kingdom of God; spend time on your knees every day before the Lord. The Lord wants your prayers so He can answer them.

There is another aspect to our prayers, and that is a prayer that removes sin and permits a work to be done in the kingdom of God. In the book of Acts, Stephen was before the council witnessing of his faith in the Lord. The council became enraged at Stephen, cast him out of the city, and began to stone him to death. Acts 7:60 says, "And he kneeled down, and cried out with a loud voice, Lord, lay not this sin to their charge. And when he had said this he fell asleep [Stephen died]." Stephen loosed the men who were there stoning him to death from their sin of murder.

In Matthew 18:18 Jesus says, "Verily I say unto you, Whatsoever ye shall bind here on the earth shall be bound in heaven; and whatsoever ye shall loose on earth it shall be loosed in heaven." Stephen loosed the men from their sin of murder. Stephen loosed the men from the consequences of their sin of killing him. Maybe all the men who stoned Stephen had that sin removed from them that day, and they would not have this sin laid to their charge by God. But there was one man there in that group who stoned Stephen that Stephen's prayer may have had profound effect on.

In verses Acts 7:58 and 8:1, a young man named Saul is mentioned who later became known as Paul. Paul was watching the clothes of the people who were about to stone Stephen. Acts 8:1 says, "And Saul was consenting unto his death ..." Saul was probably cheering on the people who were stoning Stephen. But by Stephen's prayer, Stephen released Paul from the sin of murder. Saul (Paul) was loosed from having Stephen's blood on his hands. Would Jesus have appeared to Paul with that sin on him while Paul was traveling on the road to Damascus (Acts 9:1–22)? Did Stephen's prayer loosening Paul from his sin give Jesus some sort of spiritual release to appear to Saul on the Damascus road and use Paul in the way that He did in all that Paul did to further the gospel and write half the New Testament? I think that it is entirely possible.

Most Christians know that the stain of some sin in our lives prevents God from moving as He would like. Stephen's prayer loosening Paul from that sin helped the kingdom of God to be expanded. Forgiveness and prayer loosening people from their sin and offenses become a weapon in our spiritual warfare to further the kingdom. Little did Stephen realize in his prayer of forgiveness for the men stoning him seconds before his death that God would later use one of those men to greatly further His kingdom. Stephen's prayer had future consequences for Paul to be saved, preach the gospel, and write much of the New Testament. When we hold onto unforgiveness, we are forbidding the furtherance of God's kingdom on the earth. God, help us to daily forgive others for their offenses against us, and use our forgiveness of others as spiritual warfare to further Your kingdom.

CHAPTER 16
How to Study Bible Prophecy with Purpose

G o into any Bible bookstore and you will see plenty of books about Bible prophecy on the shelves. Some of these books have a chapter on how to study Bible prophecy to help their readers understand the basics of proper Bible prophecy exegesis. There are certain rules to apply to the Scriptures in gaining a proper knowledge of what is being studied.

They mention things like expositional constancy, where if something is portrayed constantly in a certain way through the law, the prophets, and the gospels, it will be applied in the same way in the prophetic writings. For instance, if the nation of Israel is pictured symbolically as a fig tree in the law, which are the first five books of the Bible, and then it is pictured as the fig tree in the historical books, such as 1 and 2 Samuel, 1 and 2 Kings, and 1 and 2 Chronicles, etc., then it is pictured the same way in the prophetic writings and the gospels, then whenever we see the fig tree mentioned in Revelation, we can with assurance say that the text is talking about the nation of Israel. There are certain rules that have been created over the years to expound Bible study for maximum benefit. Some of these interpretive rules follow a certain teaching for a group or denomination to preserve a doctrine for that particular group of believers.

These books will also mention literal and symbolic ways to follow in our Bible prophecy interpretations. They may say that we must interpret end times Scriptures as literally or symbolically as possible whenever we can to help us understand what the Scripture is saying in its proper context.

There are many methods used to interpret Bible prophecy. Some are good and some are not. The overwhelmingly worst way to interpret Bible prophecy is to pull one Scripture out of the Word and build a huge doctrine upon it that doesn't align with any other Scripture. You may recall the Children of God cult doing this same thing. They pulled out one thread from the tapestry of the Bible and built up a huge doctrine on it, and that doctrine didn't line up with anything the rest of the Bible says. The result of applying an interpretive rule properly to any Scripture is that the result must be in agreement with all other Scriptures in the Bible.

Now while the books on Bible prophecy may offer good ways to interpret end-times prophecy, there is another way to interpret Bible prophecy that is in line with God's purpose for prophecy. It is very simple and easy to understand. This way of interpretation doesn't take a degree from a Bible school or years of study. This particular way to interpret prophecy is to see it from God's side. It is not the only way to interpret Bible prophecy, but it certainly is a way that helps us see God's purpose for prophecy. Most interpretive rules and guidelines that Bible interpreters use have a statement saying how to use that rule to interpret a Scripture, like the expositional constancy rule. Seeing God's purpose for prophecy is no different. The way to follow in the interpretation of God's purpose for prophecy is this: Always look to see how God is creating and deepening relationships with people through prophecy.

For an example of this, let's look at the deliverance of the children of Israel from their hard bondage in Egypt. Egypt was an ancient superpower. It is safe to say that what happened in Egypt was broadcast around the known world at that time. Something as big as several million slaves being delivered by God would be huge news around the world.

Many details would've been known by travelers, business people, and statesmen in Egypt, and the news of what God had done would be brought back by them to their own countries. The magnitude of this story would be around for centuries and the details of it talked about in other countries. Now it would be impossible to know the number of people who may have come to faith around the world because of what God did in Egypt. Even the Egyptians must've thought, *Our gods are nothing like the God of the Hebrew slaves*, maybe even to the point of following the true God because He had proven He is God.

When God does something, it prospers in the purpose He uses it for. It overflows in what it was meant to do. The Bible doesn't say how many people may've come have faith in other countries because of this story, but it was a huge story for the time. We still talk about 9/11, and it will be quite a while before we forget that date. The whole world knew that the World Trade Center was attacked on that date. What did all the ancient people in Africa think who heard of this strange story of deliverance from bondage by God? Everyone in Africa would likely have known about the Hebrew slaves in Egypt and how the Egyptians prospered because of them.

The Israelites' deliverance must have been a powerful story told time and again by travelers who had seen it happen. Some of the people who heard of it may've decided to have faith in this all-powerful God. With certainty some of the bystanders in Pharaoh's court who saw these things come to pass decided to start faith in the Lord God. It is safe to say that many people whose names are not a part of the Bible story decided to have faith in the God of the Hebrews and follow the Lord God. God increased faith in the Jews and may've birthed faith in some of the Egyptians, as well as many others around the world in that time. Look for God building relationship with everyone through not only prophecy but in everything He does.

Often I find that people read their Bibles and read through prophecy and not know that they have just read a prophecy. Many prophecies in the Bible do not start with that special prophetic saying of, "Thus saith the Lord," like the prophets said before speaking the words God wanted them to say. Many people don't know that "the meek will inherit the earth" is a prophecy. We must first be able to identify prophecy in our Bible. Often a simple way to identify prophecy is to look for two words that are both in the future in the verse that may be speaking about a prophecy. The two words are "will" and "shall." Whenever you see either of those two words in any Scripture, you can examine that verse a bit more closely for possible prophetic content. Of course, those two words are used many times without prophetic meaning, but you get the idea. Just be careful to not imply meanings that aren't there.

Remember the purpose? First God's purpose for prophecy is to create and deepen relationships with people. "By prophecy God is doing something that we cannot do, and that is to tell the future so that in seeing fulfillment in His words, we will know first that He exists, and second, we are also drawn to Him in trust and faith, and the result is relationship." By prophecy God creates desire in us to know the only one who knows everything about the future. The way to interpret God's purpose for prophecy is to look for the relationships it creates. How did the fulfillment affect the people who heard it? Did it change the hearts of people when they saw the fulfillment?

In many of the Bible stories, there are bystanders like the average Egyptians who were watching the events of the story unfold. There are many people who saw the mighty things God did, yet the Bible focuses on the main characters in the story. I sometimes wonder what the common people of Egypt thought when they first heard of the prophecies of each of the ten plagues and then saw each one of the ten plagues come as predicted.

The story of Jonah as shown in many children's books on the Bible is mostly about the prophet being swallowed by a great fish. But you know that is not the main theme of the story. The heart of the story is how God created relationship with a whole city by reaching them with a prophetic warning of destruction delivered by Jonah. Did the people of Nineveh initiate the relationship with God? No! They were too content to continue in their great sin. It was God who reached out to Nineveh to create relationship with that city and save an entire city, from the king to the least person living there. The Bible says the city of Nineveh had a population of one hundred and twenty thousand, and the text may indicate that the actual number may've been close to six hundred thousand. As many as six hundred thousand people were saved not only from their city's destruction, but they also were saved by God individually for eternity. The Lord started relationship with the very sinful people of Nineveh with words about their future.

With this view of prophecy, there in no need to set aside or change any of your doctrine to use this "new" method of interpretation. There is no school to go to so you can learn this "new" way of Bible interpretation. There is no college degree needed to understand this way of interpretation. However, when you interpret Bible prophecy in this way, you will be drawn to see the Lord, who shows His faithfulness, His longsuffering, His glory, and most of all His great desire to be close to us forever.

No verse has to be taken out of context to be the foundation for a huge and false doctrine. There is no date setting, no offense, and no weird, media-generated image that we cringe at being associated with. This way of Bible prophecy interpretation supplements any belief and doctrine you may have about the end times. It may not validate your view, but it will glorify God, and as we see God glorified, we are drawn to Him all the more. God filled His Word with so much prophecy to prove He exists to create and deepen relationships with everyone. It is just that simple and easy to understand. Bible prophecy must point us to Jesus and His great love for us; if our interpretations do anything less and our interpretations glorify some person, doctrine, or end-times horror, that causes fear and does not glorify the one who wrote it, and that is poor teaching.

As I have stated before, if I had a choice between understanding all the end-times prophecies exactly as they will play out or understanding God's purpose for prophecy, it would be a quick and easy choice. I'd choose knowing God's purpose for prophecy. Knowing what will happen is special, but having relationship is better than knowing about events. Understanding His purpose for prophecy is where I am drawn closer to the Lord, my God. Knowing the Scriptures on the end times is good, as it is to know all Scripture. I'm not trying to play one part of Scripture against another, but our study of prophecy must not stop with the end times. We must go on and see God's purpose for it. Someone may know Bible prophecy backward and forward, but that can cause endless debates with opposing views instead creating of a closer walk with the Lord. Seeing God's purpose for prophecy creates unity and draws us closer to Him.

I have been involved in studying Bible prophecy for many years, and I have seen firsthand the debates that this subject can produce. It is not glorifying to God, and we must change our view it in a way that unifies us instead of something that at times has divided us into doctrinally opposed groups. My intent has not been to write this book to change people's beliefs to accept my doctrine on the end times. I know my own doctrine has slipped in; please forgive me. But I teach from what I know, and what I know helps to explain the purpose for prophecy. My intent has been to help people see that the church is in a rut regarding our teaching on prophecy and to help people to know that there is a larger picture to see.

It is not that teaching on Bible prophecy is bad, but it is like driving in only one crowded lane of a superhighway with all the other lanes wide open. Let's use all the lanes of that superhighway for maximum benefit of what the highway was built for. You'll still get to where you are going in that crowded lane, but why not use an open and free lane? Understanding God's purpose for prophecy helps our faith to grow, and it doesn't change anyone's doctrine. It is like giving a plant fertilizer to make it grow larger and become more fruitful. The fertilizer doesn't change the plant into some other plant; it just helps the plant grow up strong and healthy.

Look at Just One of Our Benefits

This book discusses the purpose of prophecy; there are many benefits from prophecy, but we have to discuss how to study the benefits from prophecy to help understand the many facets of the purpose. God tells us about future events. God also tells us about future rewards and benefits given for a life of faith, but the ultimate benefit is being close to Him. Sure, we will have eternal life, resurrection from the dead, and so on. Those are great things, and they are things that we place our hope in. They are better things than anything on earth, but the best benefit of all is in knowing Him and experiencing the depth of His love.

Let's take one of the wonderful benefits that God will give us because of our faith in Him and discover how that benefit is given to us. Philippians 3:21 says, "Who [God] shall change our vile body, that it may be fashioned like unto his glorious body, according to the working whereby he is able even to subdue all things unto himself." First Corinthians 15:53 says, "For this corruptible must put on incorruption, and this mortal must put on immortality." Revelation 21:4 says, "And God shall wipe away all tears from their eyes; and there shall be no more death, neither sorrow, nor crying, neither shall there be any more pain: for the former things are passed away." In these three Scriptures, we see that we will receive new eternal bodies that will never feel pain or sorrow and never have a need to cry. Our bodies feel pain and sorrow all the time and all the more pain as we age. But God promises us new bodies, eternal bodies that will not grow old, slow down with age, or cause us to lose our minds with Alzheimer's disease. It is an extreme hope, and it is a much better than a hope in anything in this world.

Animals like dogs and cats do not live as long as people. When children experience the death of an animal, they wish that their pets could live as long as they do. They don't want their pets to die. Our bodies grow old and die. We need new bodies to live forever. God wants us with Him forever because He loves us, so He gives us eternal bodies that will never die so that we can be with Him forever and He can love on us for eternity.

We've all been some place we don't care for and wished that we could leave as soon as possible. It is also true that we have all been some place we love and don't ever want to leave. When God gives us new eternal bodies so that we can live with Him forever, it shows His love for us. He never wants to lose us because we grow old and die. Giving us eternal bodies shows He wants to spend eternity with us. You really have to love someone a lot to spend all eternity with him or her; that's the depth of His love. Amazing, isn't it? Giving eternal life to those He loves is showing love to those He gives eternal life. Giving eternal life is a benefit born from His love for us.

Losing What You Have to Obtain That Which You Cannot Lose

God is righteous. God is holy. God is all knowing. God knows we need motivational benefits to live a life of faith in Him. We need these benefits to produce hope that we can overcome our human nature's love of sin. Galatians 5:24 says, "And they that are Christ's have crucified the flesh with the affections and lusts." Matthew 10:39 says, "He that findeth his life shall lose it: and he that loseth his life shall find it." Finally Romans 12:1 says, " I beseech you therefore brethren, by the mercies of God that ye present your bodies a living sacrifice, holy, acceptable unto God which is your reasonable service."

God asks us to crucify the flesh, lose our lives for His sake, and present our bodies as a living sacrifice unto God. Who would lead a life that requires all this without the hope of receiving extreme benefits? What do I get that is better than what I have to give up? Certainly a bank robber won't go into a bank and demand that a teller give him ten cents and be happy on his way out the door that he robbed a bank to get ten cents. No! The risk of robbing a bank is too great to get caught and be sent to prison. The bank robber wants to get as much cash as he can before heading out of the bank to make his getaway. We don't have the risk that a bank robber has, but our whole lives have value to us, and we wouldn't want to squander it on something that won't be worthwhile.

Remember our example of the medical school student? The student attends eight or more years of college with the hope of being a medical doctor upon graduation. No medical student with that much learning hopes to work at a hospital only to empty bedpans for minimum wages. The reward you receive must be greater than what you have to do or give up to obtain that which you hope for. Our rewards and benefits that come from God are extreme.

Our hope in this life is only to gain more stuff and have a good life. That is a life that depends on chance or good fortune. If your health is good, you know the right people, and have enough money, the right education, or a good skill at something, then you can have a good life. It depends on where you live, what caste you come from, or what side of the tracks you were born on. It depends on how events happen, being in the right place at the right time, or how many life boats were on the Titanic. An athlete is only an athlete as long as his or her body is able to compete at the highest level. We are all amazed over the salaries of the top athletes, but they only compete at that level for a few years before their bodies give out and they can't compete anymore.

We look at movie stars as having a glamorous life. They are popular and have fan clubs, but the Bible says favor is deceitful and beauty is vain (Prov. 31:30). Having all your hope in these things is pretty dismal. You might as well put all your hope in what a fortune cookie says. God knows our human nature is eager to sin, and therefore He gives us extraordinary benefits to overcome our human nature's sinful desires and to become His servants in the hope of obtaining all that He has prophesied/promised.

When you study God's benefits for you and read a Scripture that mentions a future benefit for your faith, then you will know that they are God's own promises for your future that He has made directly to you. Promises are the standard for the words God speaks to us. We will receive it in due time, but it is a benefit for our future. We live our lives in hope of getting what has been promised. Study your Bible to see all the benefits, and be aware of the benefits that start as prophecies. Of course the indwelling of the Holy Spirit, which is a benefit that we enjoy now, started as words about the future from Jesus (John 14:16–17 15:26, 16:7–13). The benefits are the source of our hope in Christ.

If you met a rich man in a restaurant and he didn't promise you anything and just expressed regret over your financial situation and left, then he wouldn't have given you any hope for your finances by saying he would help you out. You would only be able to tell your friends that you had met this wealthy person, and that would a bit exciting, but it wouldn't give you hope for your personal situation. The same is true for our faith in the Lord. If God gave no benefits, we wouldn't have cause for hope. But if you met the rich man and he promised to greatly help your financial situation, then you have great cause for hope. The same is true with the things God has promised us to bring us into faith and relationship.

So simply look into God's Word and see how much He desires to be in relationship with the whole world by studying a part of God's relationship-building process called prophecy. In time He will show His tenderness for you and His desire to be with you forever, He will show you His grace for you and His total love for you throughout His Word

You are beginning a new path of understanding of what we call prophecy. You are coming out of the ruts that have been a familiar way of understanding this subject for a long time. Don't forget about the end-times teachings because they are a part of all the prophecies in your Bible, but go on in your understanding to see God's purpose for all Bible prophecy.

God deeply desires that we have fellowship with Him, and prophecy is one of the ways God reaches out to us to bring us close.

CHAPTER 17

The Conclusion

B y now you can see that God's main purpose for prophecy is to create and deepen relationships. God's purpose for prophecy is to draw us into relationship and bless us with its many benefits. God knows what is best for us because He designed us with an intrinsic need to know Him. He loves us. Through repetitive examples, the Bible shows that our hope is rooted in the things God has told us that we will receive for our faith. Those things are promises with a future fulfillment. Those promises create a strong hope, and a strong hope defeats fear and despair. Hope keeps us going when things look dark and dismal. We hope in those precious and fantastic words that detail what we will receive because of our faith.

The promises God gives are more precious than anything on this earth. We derive hope from those promises, and that produces an equally precious hope. Hope strengthens faith that enables us to crucify the flesh and lose our lives in order to obtain those promises. Hope readies us for kingdom service, just like gassing up the car before a long trip. That is why there are so many benefits for a Christian's faith in Christ. Of course we enjoy some of the benefits here now, but our hope expects to receive things like salvation, forgiveness, eternal life, a place in heaven with the Lord, a new body, and all of the things on the benefits list.

Prophecy is inescapable when we read the words of God. From prophetic witnessing to prophetic prayers, strengthening our faith, giving us confidence in our hope in Christ, and so on, prophecy is like the salt in sea water. It's everywhere in the Scriptures, and clearly its benefits are so awesome. We find Bible prophecy in the most unlikely of places in the Bible, such as in the Lord's Prayer, in the Sermon on the Mount, in the Beatitudes, in Peter's speech in the second chapter of Acts, and even in John 3:16. Prophecy is in every book of the Bible and is so much a part of our life in Christ. Many of the Bible stories were started by a prophecy from God.

I repeated a saying throughout this book that I think is very true, and you will remember that it says this: "By prophecy God does something that we can't do, that is to tell the future, so that when we see the fulfillment, we will realize that He exists and we will be drawn to know more about Him in faith and trust. The result is relationship."

When God created us, I think He had a purpose in mind when He decided not to give us the power to know about the future. He reserved that ability for Himself alone. The purpose in that is to prove who He is to draw us into relationship. He knew before anything was created that man would forget about Him. We would ignore His Word, His law, His loving kindness, and His great love. Entire cultures and nations have ignored Him and worshipped other gods. Generations of people have grown up in those cultures completely ignorant of the work of Jesus on the cross. He needed more to prove Himself to us and to those cultures, and He chose prophecy to fill that purpose. "Herein is love, not that we loved God, but that he loved us, and sent his Son to be the propitiation for our sins" (1 John 4:10).

God is reaching out to everyone with the power of His Word, all of it in the hope of bringing everyone close to Him. He is loving, and His mercies endure forever. He is very willing that none should perish. In Hebrews 10:7, Paul quotes Psalm 40:7 when he says, "Then said I, Lo, I come (in the volume of the book it is written of me,) to do thy will, O God." Jesus came doing God's will as it was prophesied about

Him. The prophecies Jesus fulfilled are still testifying, still proving, and still reaching out to pull on people's hearts and bring them into intimacy with Him.

We as the church have come so far from knowing and benefiting from the purpose of Bible prophecy. It's like the church has traveled to a faraway place, away from prophecy, but we can fix that. We can come back to where we were in God's Word. It is so easy; just read the Word and learn from it. Let it saturate your mind, and keep an eye out for the prophetic. Like riding a bicycle for the first time, you have to try to keep your balance, pedal, steer to make it go where you want, obey the laws, and look out for cars on the road. Doing all those things every second while riding the bike seems impossible at first, but when you keep riding, you get the hang of it. In time it becomes second nature. Studying prophecy is the same first-time-doing-it kind of thing. It may seem strange at first, but in time it will become second nature to you.

I feel strongly that the most important thing about prophecy is not about fitting every verse into its proper place in Bible end-times prophecy; it is searching the Scriptures to see how much God loves us and desires to create and deepen relationships with us. That is my goal when I study prophecy now, and it is much more beneficial for my faith. We must take prophecy from the external—the events of the end times—to make it internal to see the purpose He intended. Those things are the relationship, the hope, and the empowerment prophecy brings to the life of every believer.

I must admit that there has been a pendulum shift in my view of prophecy since I discovered that God had a purpose for prophecy. Sometimes studying the end times has been somewhat of an intellectual exercise for me as I study all the interpretations and try to properly apply them. Learning about God's purpose for prophecy to fulfill His Word and prove that He is real to me brings me to trust Him more. That is better for me than when I am just doing research about the coming one-world

government, the Antichrist, or Armageddon. There have been no books
I've studied that talk about God having a purpose for prophecy, no great
volume of sermons to draw from and learn these things; it has been my
own learning curve. When I learned that of all the verses in the Bible,
over one quarter were prophetic, I just asked the question, "Lord, why
did You relate so much of Your Word to us in a way that tells the
future?" You are holding in your hands the answer to that question. I
just knocked, and He opened the door. These three books say so much
more about Him than it does about any person.

When we talk about the end times, we externalize the things that will
happen into events. Events can be examined and debated. Not to
minimize any portion of Scripture, but we need to see more than that
part of the prophetic picture. When we learn about God's purpose
for prophecy, we look at all prophecy and go internal with what the
prophetic fulfillments do inside of us. That is the main reason for all
prophecy. The fourth element of prophecy is so important because it is
the internal work in our hearts. That is where God sends His Word to
do the work in our hearts.

Isaiah 55:11 says, "So shall my word be that goeth forth out of my
mouth: it shall not return unto me void, but it shall accomplish that
which I please, and it shall prosper in the thing whereto I sent it."
God's Word includes a lot of prophecy to prove who He is so we will
be drawn to Him in faith. The thing that is accomplished according
to what pleases God is His Word in our hearts to drawing us to Him.
Relationship born out of faith is the thing God sends His Word out
to accomplish in our hearts. After seeing fulfillment and knowing that
God is real, the heart takes over, and it has decisions to make. God
doesn't want us to dismiss it as coincidence. He wants us to decide to
have faith. It is then that we are drawn to the one who knows the future,
and relationship starts.

I know I have been quite subject singular in this book in mentioning that we come to the Lord through prophecy. I know that the goodness of God also leads us to repentance, as Romans 2:4 says. Please believe me—I am not so wrapped up in the purpose for prophecy that I don't see any other way to God. I know there are many things God uses to reach people, and I believe that with all my heart. But everything that God does is done to bring us into a close fellowship, and to miss that one major point is to miss out on all that He intended for us to enjoy from the benefits of prophecy.

I also know that I have been repetitive. I am sorry for that, but it was very intentional. It is like the elementary school flash card to help learn basic arithmetic. But in the case of prophecy, the flash cards of reminders had to keep coming to help change the cemented in equation that prophecy equals the end times. The repetitive reminders had to keep coming to not only unlearn a long-time habit but to learn a new way of looking at prophecy.

Simmering on the Back Burners

I confess that I don't understand everything about the Bible or about prophecy even though I have been studying it for many years. There are many questions I have about Bible prophecy. I have a place in my mind that I call the back burner. If I don't understand something, I send it to the back burner and let it simmer there. It sits there until I get more information or gain more insight about what I don't understand. What I can't define may sit on that back burner until I meet Jesus. I don't try to define what I don't understand. That leads to false teaching and doctrine. I don't worry about it; I trust that God will give me the answers, either in this life or the next.

When I was in my ninth-grade math class, they started mixing letters in with the numbers. They called it algebra, and I called it gibberish. I thought numbers were for math and letters were for spelling. How could they mix these two together? I didn't understand it at all. I went for extra help, but my math teacher said she was too busy to give me any extra help. Algebra went straight to that back burner, and it's been there ever since. I don't have to understand everything. It is enough for me to be patient and wait for understanding, and I can do that. If I'm not so sure about something, you will probably hear me say that it is a back-burner issue. It's not because it's unimportant; it's just that understanding or defining it may be difficult. We can't completely define every Bible verse, so we need those back burners.

It is very important that you do not commit yourself to believing in some new doctrine. Hold fast to the things you know to be true, but when you hear a new doctrine, test it, try it, and see if it fits in with the rest of Scripture. Most of the time when you hear something completely new, it is time to put the brakes on, put the red flags up, slow down, and start talking with other believers who read the Word a lot so it can be examined carefully, with lots of study. I hope that the church will closely scrutinize what this book says to see if what I am saying is true or the babblings of deception. Interpreting Scriptures safely means looking at the whole Word of God to compare something new you hear to all Scripture to see if it is true. Cults are usually started by lone wolves who are not in community and not in a place where there is submission to others in a church. They misinterpret some Scripture and start preaching it and draw a following after themselves. If it is not aligned with all Scripture, then it is false. It is just that simple. Why would God say something in one century and contradict it in another? That would not make any sense. Remember, everything will be revealed some day. *Everything* will be revealed, and that even includes the gibberish they call algebra.

Starting a New Obedience

I encourage you to start your own study of prophecy based on your obedience in Christ. You will be like those two righteous people, Simeon and Anna, in Luke 2:25–39. They were watching for fulfillment of prophecy. Jesus told us ten times in the New Testament to watch. You and I both know that watching is looking at prophecy to see it comes to be fulfilled. You will have an understanding of Bible prophecy in time.

Reading the daily newspapers or watching the TV news will take on a whole different purpose for you. Together with your new knowledge of prophecy, you will be looking for signs and fulfillment. If there is a prophetic fulfillment, you will know it because of your knowledge of the Bible. You will be just like Anna and Simeon, keeping a watch for fulfillment, although in this day and age you will be looking for different signs and fulfillments than Anna and Simeon looked for. More than seeing the end times unfolding before your eyes, you will see the love God has for you in proving who He is to you because He first told you exactly what would happen. Mark 13:37 says, "And what I say unto you I say unto all, Watch." I think that applies to you and me.

I also caution you to be aware that you could be way out in left field with your doctrine about what is coming. Have a sense that what you believe can be modified or corrected by truthful insight at any time. Don't overly commit to anything outside of the atoning blood of Jesus' sacrifice on the cross for us. Defining every Scripture about the last days, while it has some benefits, is not like our faith in Jesus. So take it easy, especially with others who may believe differently about the end times than you. Don't draw the doctrinal boundaries around your pet theory and lob scriptural bombs at others from the confines and comfort of what you know about the end times. Doing that is not righteous or glorifying to God.

The Lord wants you to know Him and be close to Him. God wants your heart and soul to be close to Him. How can we do that when we attack others with the Scriptures? Love others by not debating them endlessly. You can beat someone over the head with what you know about prophecy, but how does that fulfill the love of God? Maturity in the Lord says you don't always have to be proven right.

Obedience to God's Word is a proper response to God once we realize who He is. He is bigger than we are, He is very powerful, and He is all knowing. We are not. He is God, not me. I can give Him the authority to lead me because I trust His loving interest in me. I can trust Him all the more because He knows the future and can protect me from harm no matter where or how that harm may come. I wonder how many times He has kept me safe while I'm driving my car and how many times He kept me safe from harm while I'm out or at home. I'm sure He will reveal all that He has done for me over my eternity with Him. I can trust a God who does that. I can obey a God who knows everything, sees every sin I have committed, and hears all I have said and still gently surrounds me with His great love.

Know Him through His Word

You may be thinking you know about the Lord but not the Lord Himself. Is the Lord is more like an acquaintance to you and not very close? If so, then you can know the Lord today. It is not difficult to know the Lord. God has made it easy to know Him. If you feel that you don't really know the Lord, then you can begin to get to know Him today. It is easy to know the Lord because He has written all about Himself in a book. He has written extensively about His likes and dislikes and His nature. He has put examples of how He has dealt with people who are in sin and with people who are obedient. He has shown you His plan for you and His promises for you in His Word. Our response to God after we have decided to have faith is to find out as much as we can about Him. There are many subjects that spark our interest: sports, history, cars, collecting something, gossip, travel, and so on. We study a lot about the things that interest us. When we realize how big God is, our response is to find out everything we can about Him so we can know Him and how we can interact with the almighty God who created this universe.

> For thus saith the high and lofty One that inhabiteth eternity, whose name is Holy; I dwell in the high and holy place, with him also that is of a contrite and humble spirit, to revive the heart of the contrite ones. (Isa. 57:15)

Over Eight Thousand Proofs

Over eight thousand prophetic verses in your Bible prove to you over ten thousand times that God is faithful to fulfill the things He says. It proves over ten thousand times that He is reaching out to be close with you. Through those ten thousand verses, He is showing you how much He wants to be with you. Maybe you've been running on empty for far too long. Please come and fill up your tank and partake of the many benefits of knowing the Lord. He wants to be with you no matter who you are, no matter what you've done, and no matter where you've been. It doesn't even matter what or how you think of yourself. God just wants to be close to you. If you have deep hurts and suffer emotional pain, then know that being close to our Savior is very healing and restorative.

If searching for a religion were like shopping for a car in a huge car lot, I think the choice would be very obvious. There would be a lot of broken down cars on this lot. You would walk around on this car lot and look at each car to buy. Some would have no engine and some would need the engine replaced every twenty thousand miles. Who would buy these cars? Some people would try to make their own cars by taking parts from other cars to build their own. Unfortunately, there would be many flaws with these cars, and they wouldn't go anywhere.

Then you would see this cherry of a car. It would be beautiful and have every imaginable option and comfort. It would be an antique classic, and it could be yours for a down payment of repentance and a daily commitment of faith. If we really compare what we believe to other religions, we have so much to hope for and so much proof for our faith. Imagine believing that you have to live many lives on this planet and go through the pain of living in this world each time. What kind of hope is that? A hope for heaven with Christ after one life lived is a much better hope than that. Prophecy helps to make faith in Jesus the best car on the lot.

> "Being born again, not of corruptible seed, but of incorruptible, by the word of God, which liveth and abideth for ever" (1 Peter 1:23).

I've had a few building projects where I built something out of wood. When I build something, it has to be as perfect as my meager woodworking skills will allow. It has to be heavy duty and very strong. I want it to last and be stronger than it needs to be. But God didn't make us this way. He made us with a flaw. He made us like a table with one leg much longer than the others. It wobbles horribly because of that one longer leg. God looks at our flaws and says, "Yup, that's just the way I designed and intended it to be."

Our flaw is a desire to sin. The consequences of our sin are to be deceived by sin, separated from God, and die spiritually to Him. You are being deceived by sin to think that based on what you have done or your perception of yourself that God wants nothing to do with you. You have to understand all that properly, without the deception affecting your perception. You think that because Satan has twisted God's design. You look at your God-given flaw and tell yourself that your flaw is the thing that keeps you from coming to God. It is a deception nurtured by Satan to make you think you will always be estranged from God. Nothing could be further from the truth. God designed your flaw to bring you to Him.

Listen to this verse out of Romans 8:20: "For the Creature [that's you] was made subject to vanity [vanity is the flaw/sin] not willingly, but by reason of him [that's God] who hath subjected the same [that's you

184

again] in hope." Your flaw is your human nature and its desire to sin. God created you with it in the hope that you would ask Him for help with it. So don't think your flaw prevents you from coming to God. God gave you that flaw in the hope of creating relationship with you.

Just as a small child lacks the ability to do many things and needs help from his parents, we all lack the ability to live without this flaw affecting us. When children realize they can't do something by themselves, they cry out for help from their parents. This is a natural response once small children realize they cannot do something on their own. God designed us with this flaw to have the same effect on us. Like the small child calls to his parents, He wants us to call out to Him. He wants us to ask Him for help. He loves us and wants to help. So whatever sin you're thinking of that you think prevents you from coming to God is actually the very thing God hopes will bring you to Him.

Don't think you have to fix the flaw before you come to Him. No! God put it there, and He has already fixed it by the cross of Jesus Christ. You just have to accept Him and believe in what He did on the cross for you. Having faith in God is the fix to the problem, so don't let Satan lie and condemn you by saying, "Look at what you have done. God won't forgive you for that." Jesus died once and for all, taking all our sin upon Him that we might be made whole. Don't let your ugly past stop your beautiful future. God does care about what we have done, but much more than that, He has made a way out of this mess so that you can be close to Him.

> He that hath my commandments, and keepeth them, he it is that loveth me: and he that loveth me shall be loved of my Father, and I will love him, and will manifest myself to him. (John 14:21)

God loves you and wants to be with you. He wants you to know Him. Jesus has removed the obstacle of sin that blocks us from being close to and knowing God. You are free to respond to God right now, holding nothing back. You can have a closeness with God today that you never thought possible before, and all it takes is an earnest prayer for your new life to begin.

A Prayer That Can Change Your Life and Your Eternity

If you desire a life in a relationship with God and also have the hope that His promises bring, then you can start on your amazing journey with God right now. All it takes is a simple prayer for all of this to start. Saying this simple prayer can start you on your way to life eternal. Think of it—you can have eternal life in a new body that never feels pain or sorrow! That and much more can be yours, but most of all, that you can know God personally. Just pray this simple prayer:

> Jesus, I ask for forgiveness for my sin. I believe that You died on the cross for my sin, and by Your death I am forgiven, accepted, and made righteous. Jesus, I believe that You that you have been raised from the dead and that You are God. I give my life to You, and I will seek to know what You want me to do. I understand that You love me and have my eternal good in Your heart for me. Help me to know You and be in close fellowship with You.

That prayer, said in honesty and sincerity, has amazingly powerful eternal consequences for you. If you said that prayer in earnest, then everything has changed for you, because now you are saved from eternal death. Sure, you still look the same on the outside, but spiritually everything about you has changed. Now you are a part of a worldwide family of people who love God and are called according to His purpose. You are now a servant of the Most High God.

Start your fellowship with God by reading the Word that He has provided for us to know him—the Bible. The Bible has answers for your faith, and it is a light for the path your life will follow. Go to a Bible-believing, Bible-preaching church where Jesus and people are loved. People aren't perfect, so there are no perfect churches—just people just like you seeking to do the will of God as much as they can. Christians often fall short of what God wants us to do, and often that falling short looks sloppy, but God is in this lifelong process to work out our salvation with Him.

Begin to pray to God. Prayers are talking with God and making requests to Him. Pray for your faith to grow and to be strengthened. Pray for God to show you how to live for Him. Pray for your friends and relatives to come to know the Lord also. Prayer is also a listening time, to listen to anything that the Lord will say to you.

Don't neglect your new life in Christ. It must be nurtured by reading the Word, by prayer, and by fellowshipping with others who know the Lord. Just like a plant needs water, soil, and sunshine to grow, you need things to grow your faith. Soon you will learn what the Lord wants you to do, and you will know Him more and more every day. You will start to experience a relationship with almighty God, and through His Word, you will see how much He loves you. Everything you once lived and hoped for pales in comparison with your relationship with God. Outwardly the life we lead here on this earth looks like anyone else's life, but inside of us is where the glory of God is. We know the immense promises of God and who we are in Christ. All these things we receive from God both now and in the next life easily surpass anything this life can offer

God bless you as you seek to know Him with your whole heart.

ABOUT THE AUTHOR

I was raised in a town on the east coast and became a Christian when I was nineteen years old. I went to church as a child, but I didn't care for it. I wanted to stay home and watch TV on Sunday mornings. The church I went to while growing up was, sadly, a dead church. I can recall in one sermon the minister was preaching about a man on a Pacific island during World War II. The man was a Japanese plane spotter. He had to avoid capture and found inner strength to continue his dangerous work reporting information about Japanese movements in his area. There was no mention of Jesus or reliance upon His direction. Trusting in the Lord was never preached that I can recall.

I had a friend who had left to join a Christian ministry in Oregon called Shiloh Youth Revival Centers. About a year later, he came back for a short visit with his family before heading back to Oregon. He told me about his new life in Christ, and during his visit, we went to a Christian coffeehouse on a Bible college campus. There were all sorts of young people there praising Jesus. They were so excited about serving the Lord. I had never seen anyone have any passion for serving the Lord or for loving each other; being religious had always seemed so dry and dreary. I didn't know that you could know the Lord personally and have a relationship with Him. I accepted the Lord during my friend's visit.

After my friend went back to continue his work in the ministry, I started to get involved in the local church and go to Bible studies. I was in a post-graduate commercial art course in a vocational school. There was a church near the school, and the janitor there was a Christian who would open the doors of the church early every morning before school for Bible studies with the high school kids. I started reading and studying the Bible for the first time.

The Bible came alive to me, and I just couldn't read it enough. I went to that Bible study at the church every morning before school and found other Bible studies somewhere around town every night. Together with a Bible study in the coffeehouse and in church on Sundays, I was going to twelve Bible studies a week. If there were some way to go to more, I would've gone to those too. I just couldn't get enough of the Word of God. Almost every verse was leaping off the pages of the Bible and into my heart. It was an amazing experience of learning about the Lord. Although my Bible reading is in a different stage now, I still look forward to reading the Word every day. The Bible is never old or out of touch, and I learn something new just about every time I read it. I just love the way God's Word lives and breathes newness of life into me every time I seek Him out in it.

Over a year later, the 1973 Yom Kippur War broke out in the Middle East between Egypt, Syria, and Israel. Information about the war was in the news every day. Somehow I believed there was a connection between the Israel I was reading about in my Bible to the Israel I was reading about in the newspapers. I knew so little about the Bible then or how much connection there is between the Israel of the past to the Israel of today. I started reading everything I could about the war and what was happening there. I dove into the Scriptures to read about prophecy. That was the first serious study on Bible prophecy I had done, and it started a lifelong interest in it. We all thought the Lord's return was so close then, and I still think that way, maybe even more so now.

I do not profess to be a writer or having gone to college to study English. What I write is with the rudimentary and mostly forgotten high school–level English skills that I still possess. But I do profess a lifelong love of God and my Lord and Savior Jesus Christ. I have a passion for studying God's Word and for studying those words spoken in prophecy.

In 1996, I was able to go on my first trip to Israel. After returning from that trip, I started the Israel Night Bible Study and taught it in my church and in various groups around my hometown. We watched the excellent film series from Focus on the Family called "That the World May Know." After watching one of the short archeology-based segments on Israel, I would speak on some aspect of Bible prophecy. I assigned reading and a little homework to the people who attended. It was hard to cram all the information I had on Bible prophecy into ten weekly Bible studies, but it worked out well and people learned about Bible prophecy.

I turned my attention to writing, and I have written a large manuscript on the end times with my own version of interpretation and application. The Lord showed me that the manuscript I had written, with all its interpretation and application, wasn't the work or the timing that He wanted. *God's Purpose for Prophecy* is the work the Lord wanted me to write. I wrote *God's Purpose for Prophecy*, but it was too big and had too many subjects. Upon good and wise advice, [7] I did a rewrite of the one book into three books on prophecy, each containing a differing look at the purposes of prophecy in the life of the believer.

I believe that God has guided me through the difficult work of writing. I spent many countless hours at the computer learning as I was writing. Sometimes I would wake from sleep in the middle of the night and have a word from the Lord to get dressed, go to the computer, and write. Sometimes while I was in church, the pastor would be speaking about something and I would get a word from the Lord about the things I was writing about. I'd quickly jot down a note and continue to listen to the sermon. Something in the pastor's sermon got things going, and there would be a few more paragraphs of inspiration.

I felt compelled to write this book about prophecy, unlike the first manuscript that gives my opinions on all the end-times Scriptures, just like so many other books on the subject. I believe that God's purpose for prophecy is different than what our purpose for it has become. I have come to understand this only in the last few years, but it is right, and I know it is from the Lord. I have never heard a preacher or pastor mention anything about God having a purpose for prophecy, so I had to write this book. It was needed. Like Moses and Paul, I wish that all God's people were familiar with prophecy and could experience the benefits that come from it. I think that understanding the purpose for the one quarter of the Bible that this subject covers is foundational for all interpretation and application of Bible prophecy. The purpose writers and speakers on prophecy should have is to draw people into faith and deepen the faith of people who already believe.

It is my hope and prayer for you that you will come to a more intimate and active relationship with your almighty Creator. Since God loves you so much and greatly desires to be in an active and close fellowship with you, won't you give Him your life and see that He has your best interest close to His own heart? He shows us this great love for us through His every expression and word.

I claim no credit for this work. All the credit goes to the Lord, for He is the one who loves me with His great and amazing love. Everything else pales in comparison to being in that wonderful fellowship with Him. He is the one who has forgiven me of my great weight of sin and gives me a place in His kingdom. It is my prayer that through the Holy Spirit you will see Jesus in all that has been written here and in so doing our Father will be glorified. God bless you.

FOOTNOTES

Footnote 1: [on page ix] Time LaHaye, Prophecy Study Bible by AMG Publishers 2000 page 1421.

Footnote 2: [on page ix] Dr. David Jeremiah, Prophecy Answer Book, Published by Tomas Nelson Publishers, 2010

Footnote 3: Tim LaHaye Prophecy Study Bible by AMG Publishers, 2000, page [x].

Footnote 4: [on page 24] Tim LaHaye, Prophecy Study Bible, by AMG Publishers, 2000 Page vii Preface

Footnote 5: Watchtower October 1879, [Page 84] Zion's Watchtower January 1886 Watchtower Reprints 1, page 817; The Time is at Hand 1888 page 76-77; Watchtower July 15, 1894 Reprints Page 1677; Watchtower reprints VI Sept 1 1917 Page 5527; The Time is at Hand 1889, 1915 edition page 39;

Footnote: 6: Webster's seventh New Collegiate Dictionary, G. & C. Merriam Company, Publishers [Page 147]

Footnote 7: Professor Lee at New Hope College, Eugene, Oregon [Page 191]